Mel Bay Presents

50 Tunes for Banjo
Traditional, Old Time, Bluegrass & Celtic Solos
Volume 1

By Mark Geslison

Additional titles in this series:
99938BCD 50 Tunes for Fiddle • 99940BCD 50 Tunes for Bass
99941BCD 50 Tunes for Guitar • 99942BCD 50 Tunes for Mandolin

CD contents

<table>
<tr><td>CD 1</td><td>CD 2</td><td>CD 3</td></tr>
<tr><td>1 Angus Campbell</td><td>1 Forked Deer</td><td>1 Red-haired Boy</td></tr>
<tr><td>2 Arkansas Traveler</td><td>2 Gardenia Waltz</td><td>2 Red Wing</td></tr>
<tr><td>3 Aura Lee</td><td>3 Grandfather's Clock</td><td>3 Sailor's Hornpipe/College Hornpipe</td></tr>
<tr><td>4 The Battle Cry of Freedom</td><td>4 Green Willis</td><td>4 Saint Anne's Reel</td></tr>
<tr><td>5 Beaumont Rag</td><td>5 Indian's Farewell Waltz</td><td>5 Sally Ann</td></tr>
<tr><td>6 Billy in the Lowground</td><td>6 Irish Washerwoman</td><td>6 Sally Goodin'</td></tr>
<tr><td>7 Blackberry Blossom</td><td>7 La Bastringue</td><td>7 Sally Johnson</td></tr>
<tr><td>8 Bonaparte's Retreat</td><td>8 Leather Britches</td><td>8 Salt Creek</td></tr>
<tr><td>9 Carthage Waltz</td><td>9 Liberty</td><td>9 Soldier's Joy</td></tr>
<tr><td>10 Cherokee Shuffle</td><td>10 Martin's Waltz</td><td>10 Swallowtail Jig</td></tr>
<tr><td>11 Cluck Old Hen</td><td>11 Mason's Apron</td><td>11 Temperance Reel</td></tr>
<tr><td>12 Cotton-eyed Joe</td><td>12 Mississippi Hornpipe</td><td>12 Tom and Jerry</td></tr>
<tr><td>13 Cotton Patch Rag</td><td>13 Mississippi Sawyer</td><td>13 Turkey in the Straw</td></tr>
<tr><td>14 Cripple Creek</td><td>14 Old Dan Tucker</td><td>14 Uncle Joe</td></tr>
<tr><td>15 Devil's Dream</td><td>15 Old Joe Clark</td><td>15 Under the Double Eagle</td></tr>
<tr><td>16 Down Yonder</td><td>16 President Garfield's Hornpipe</td><td>16 Whiskey Before Breakfast</td></tr>
<tr><td>17 Eighth of January</td><td>17 Pretty Peg</td><td></td></tr>
</table>

1 2 3 4 5 6 7 8 9 0

Visit us on the Web at www.melbay.com — E-mail us at email@melbay.com

Table of Contents

*This tune is out of alphabetical order because it is the second tune of a medley.

About the Author

Mark Geslison, the author and coordinator of this series, is a multi-instrumentalist who plays the mandolin, guitar, bass, percussion, banjo and dulcimer. He has performed traditional music for most of his life and has been an instrumental champion several times since the mid-1980s including: Western Regional Guitar Champion 1988, 1989; Western Regional Mandolin Champion 1988, 1989; Utah State Guitar Champion 1988, 1989, 1992; Utah State Mandolin Champion 1988, 1989, 1992, 1994 and 2002; and Utah State Banjo Champion 2001 (4-string).

Mark has been the director of the Folk Music Ensemble program at Brigham Young University since 1992. The Folk Music Ensemble program includes performing groups that focus on Bluegrass, Appalachian, Early American and Celtic music styles. His students perform approximately one hundred times per year in all parts of the world including the South Pacific, Asia, Europe and North and South America.

Mark is also the founder and director of the Institute of American Music (IAM). IAM is a non-profit, private school of music designed to teach traditional music in an ensemble setting to young people and families. This series originated within IAM where Mark noticed a need for ensemble arrangements.

Visit...
www.instituteofamericanmusic.com

for additional products that will assist you with your study of the 50 Tunes series including:

- Curriculum books with scales, exercises, technique and graduation check-off.
- Rhythm tracks (guitar chords and metronome) for practicing all of the 50 Tunes at varying metronome speeds.
- Bluegrass and Celtic songbooks.
- Information on creating and maintaining ensembles, family bands and "communities" of music.
- Free downloads of mp3 audio tracks and pdf sheet music.

Foreword

This book contains 50 tunes from the United States, the British Isles and Canada. The companion CD set includes the recorded version of each of these 50 tunes. The appendix contains instructions on tablature reading, picking exercises, chord diagrams and chord charts. These components are designed to help you learn the enclosed fifty tunes and to promote proficiency at performing these tunes.

50 Tunes Volume 1 is not meant to be the ultimate beginning-to-advanced tool. Rather, it is intended to give a broad tune (melody) base to students and instructors alike. It is also intended to show creative arrangements of basic melodies with stylistic nuances designed to develop left and right hand skills (compare *Blackberry Blossom 1, President Garfield's Hornpipe 2* and *Salt Creek 1.*). The tunes on the CD are intended to be instructional and enjoyable at the same time.

Erik Neilson has been of vital assistance to me in creating the banjo portion of my fifty-tune project. Due to his immense contribution to this particular book, I have asked him to write the preface, acknowledgements and appendix. I know that Erik's thoughtful and well-organized approach is as good as anyone out there in banjo land. By following Erik's suggestions you will be lead in the right direction to solid banjo playing. Thanks for all the superb help, Erik.

-Mark Geslison

Preface

Welcome! Since you are reading this, you are probably looking for interesting banjo arrangements. This book, along with the other books in this series (mandolin, bass, fiddle and guitar), is designed to help you and your band, picking buddies or family in expanding your instrumental repertoire. In the following pages you will find nearly one hundred tablature arrangements for fifty traditional tunes.

This book is set up alphabetically with varying renditions of most of the tunes. These versions are generally listed in order of difficulty where '#1' represents the simpler variation while '#2' (and above) represents the more complex variation. (For example, *Temperance Reel #1* is not as difficult as *Temperance Reel #2*.) These variations range in style from the strictly melodic to the more arpeggiated "Earl Scruggs" style, but the contour of the melody should be apparent throughout. These versions allow for a certain amount of mixing and matching of licks and runs to suit your stylistic preferences. They are also designed to show the advantages and differences of the several tunings that are used. Some additional information about chords and scales in these various tunings is included in the appendix. Hopefully this will lead you to explore beyond standard G tuning and help you when arranging your own tunes from the ground up.

The appendix also includes a chord sequences section that is printed large enough to be helpful when introducing a tune to others at a jam session. Although there are no standardized 'right' versions of the chords for these tunes, those that are given will work well. They can also be altered to suit your personal harmonic preferences.

Because some of the recorded banjo parts have been arranged in various old time styles such as clawhammer and frailing, there is a bonus old time banjo section located in the appendix.

Because of the size and scope of this project, it would be impossible to include a recording of every version of every tune for every instrument on just two or three CDs. Instead, all fifty tunes are recorded at a moderate tempo with the parts being played by several instruments. This should help convey the essence of each piece while allowing you the enjoyment of playing along as you learn.

Acknowledgements

When Mark Geslison and I discussed his ideas about a one hundred-tune project several years ago, neither of us realized how time consuming such an endeavor would really be. As I write, the first fifty tunes are finally completed and it has been very satisfying to not only see the books evolve, but to work directly with Mark on many facets of this undertaking.

Mark and I first crossed paths some sixteen years ago and the results since include a number of musical highs and a lasting friendship. I appreciated Mark's tact, dedication, sense of musical vision and a sense of humor. I am grateful for the opportunity to finally see some of my musical ideas and arrangements in print. Thanks Mark.

No worthwhile project ever seems to get done without a lot of outside help. First, thanks to Valerie Johnston, my first banjo teacher, for getting me started. Second, thanks to Conley Frost, Larry Oliver, Alan Scott, Lona Hymas, Dwayne Donkersgoed and Val Sorensen, my banjo picking buddies over the years, for all their encouragement and genuine friendship.

Also, many thanks go to the banjoists over the years who have been willing to share their time and talents through recordings, concerts, workshops, Banjo Newsletter articles, books and other instructional material.

Finally, my gratitude to Rick, Dwayne, Mark, Geoff, Craig, Val and Paul for their arrangements and spirited playing on the accompanying CDs which have added so much to this project.

Finally, thanks to Bradley Slade for the photography that adds a special and professional element to this book.

-Erik Neilson

Arrangements

Rick Davis: *Cripple Creek* and *Cotton Eyed Joe* (old time section).

Rick is the city manager for West Point City, Utah by day and banjo player in a local Bluegrass band by night. He is a 2-time state banjo champion and plays both 3-finger and clawhammer styles.

Dwayne Donkersgoed: *Cotton-patch Rag #2* and *Grandfather's Clock #1*.

Dwayne is a longtime banjo player originally from Orange County, California. He is a teacher by profession, but finds enough time to maintain a small contingent of banjo students. A contributor to Banjo Newsletter (BNL.com), one of Dwayne's specialties is arranging melodies in "Travis-style" for 5-string banjo.

Mark Geslison: *Aura Lee #1*, *Carthage Waltz* and *College Hornpipe*.

Mark is a multi-instrumentalist who has won numerous contests on guitar, mandolin and, most recently, 4-string banjo (we won't hold that against him). He has also played in several successful bands including Lincoln Highway. Mark's version of *Aura Lee* is positive proof that less is more. His arrangement of *College Hornpipe* shows his ability to maintain a flowing melody without making the tune difficult to manipulate.

Geoff Groberg: *Arkansas Traveler #2*, *Leather Britches #1*, *Old Dan Tucker* (old time section), *Old Joe Clark* (old time section) and *Uncle Joe*. On *Uncle Joe* you can hear Geoff play on his hand-made, redwood head banjo. Geoff, a talented musician on a number of instruments, still maintains that the banjo is the most fun. His unique style ranges from simple frailing to sophisticated melodic arrangements.

Craig Miner: *Down Yonder* and *Grandfather's Clock #2*.

Craig is a full-time musician currently playing the role of "Banjo Boy" in the highly acclaimed contemporary Bluegrass/Pop band, Ryan Shupe and the Rubberband. He also plays guitar, mandolin and octave mandolin. Craig performs on a banjo and octave mandolin that he built. His banjo can be heard on the accompanying CD set.

Val Sorenson:

Val is a player's banjo player whose musical experimentation and composing covers interesting new territory. Val's playing on *President Garfield's Hornpipe* shows considerable ability.

Paul Washburn: *Red Wing #1* and *Salt Creek #1*.

Paul is from Sacramento, California and is a graduate of Brigham Young University. His arrangements of *Red Wing* and *Salt Creek* are both straightforward and interesting. Paul's playing can be heard on a number of tracks on the accompanying CD set.

Paul Washburn/Erik Neilson: *Red Haired Boy #1*.

Val Sorensen/Erik Neilson: *Beaumont Rag #1*.

Erik Neilson: All other arrangements.

Erik has mostly played guitar and bass in a variety of bands over the years, but the banjo is still his first love. A luthier, Erik built three banjos and one guitar used on the accompanying CD set. His construction and design ideas have led to some unusual but successful variations in traditional banjo construction. Erik has taught banjo and guitar in Idaho, Oregon and Utah during the past 25 years. It was through these years of teaching that many of the ideas presented here were developed in response to student's needs.

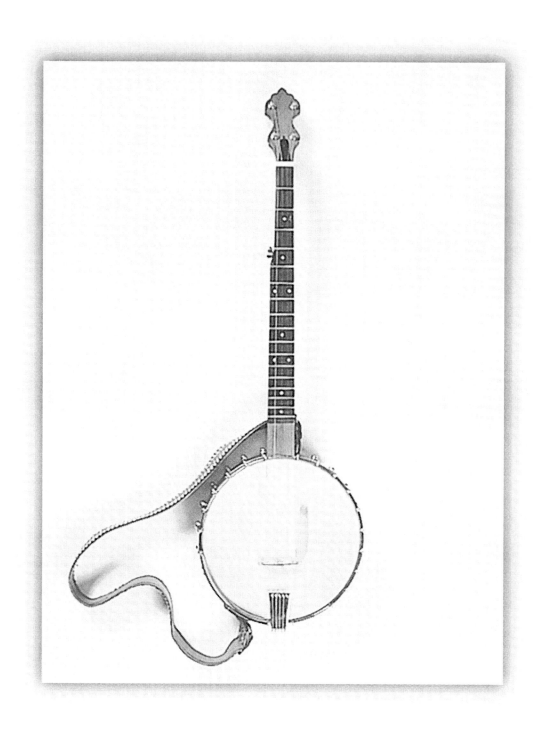

Angus Campbell

Banjo* (capo 2)

Scottish

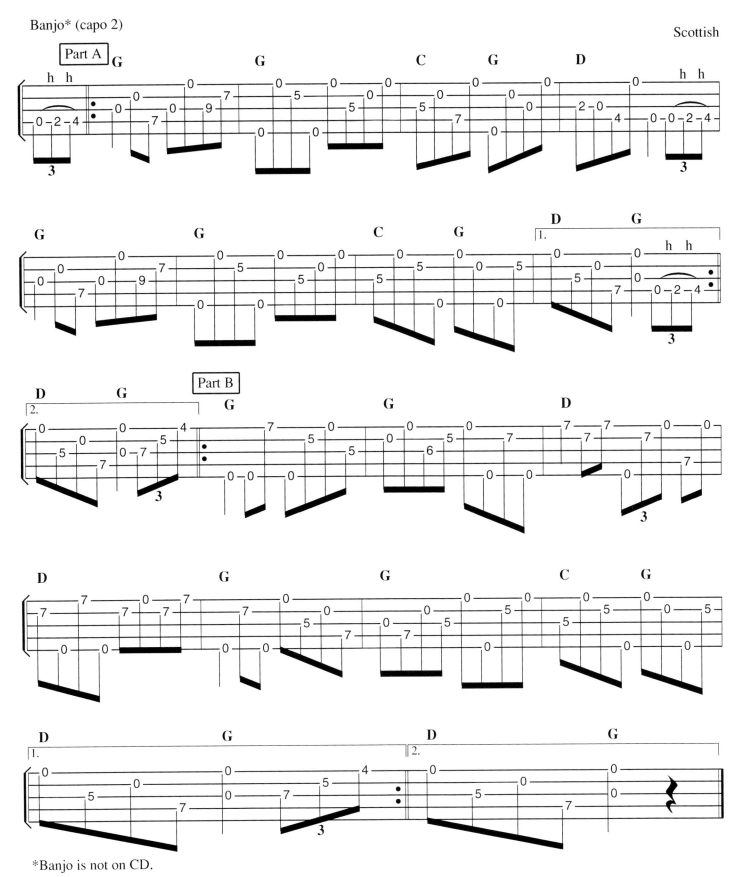

*Banjo is not on CD.

Arkansas Traveler

Banjo 1* (capo 7)

North American

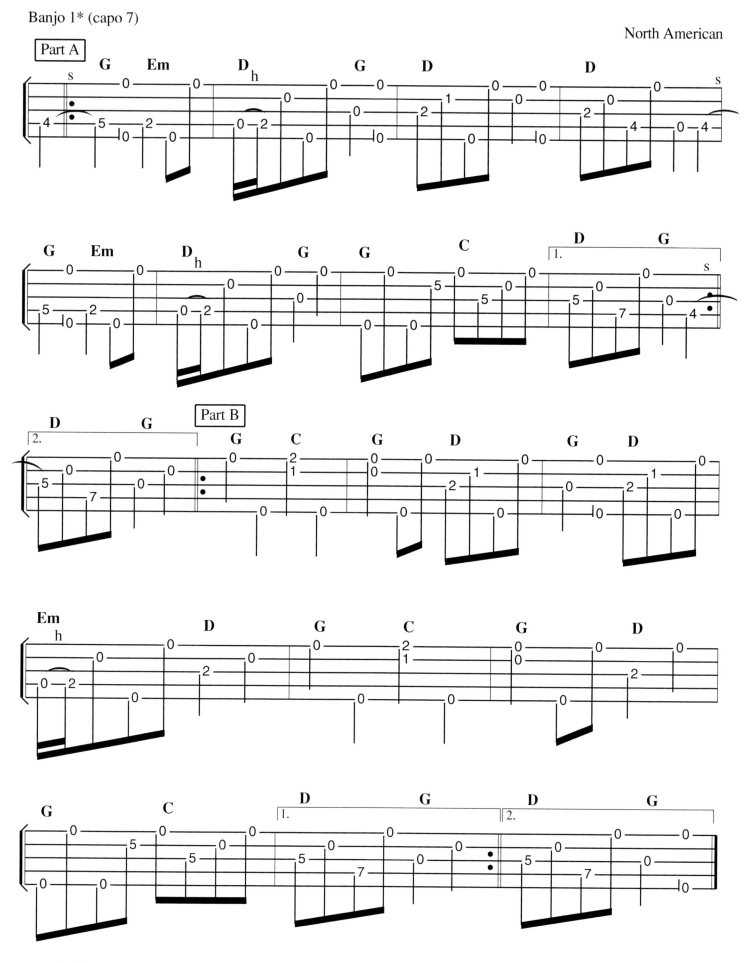

*Banjo 1 is not on CD.

Arkansas Traveler

Banjo 2 (key of G)

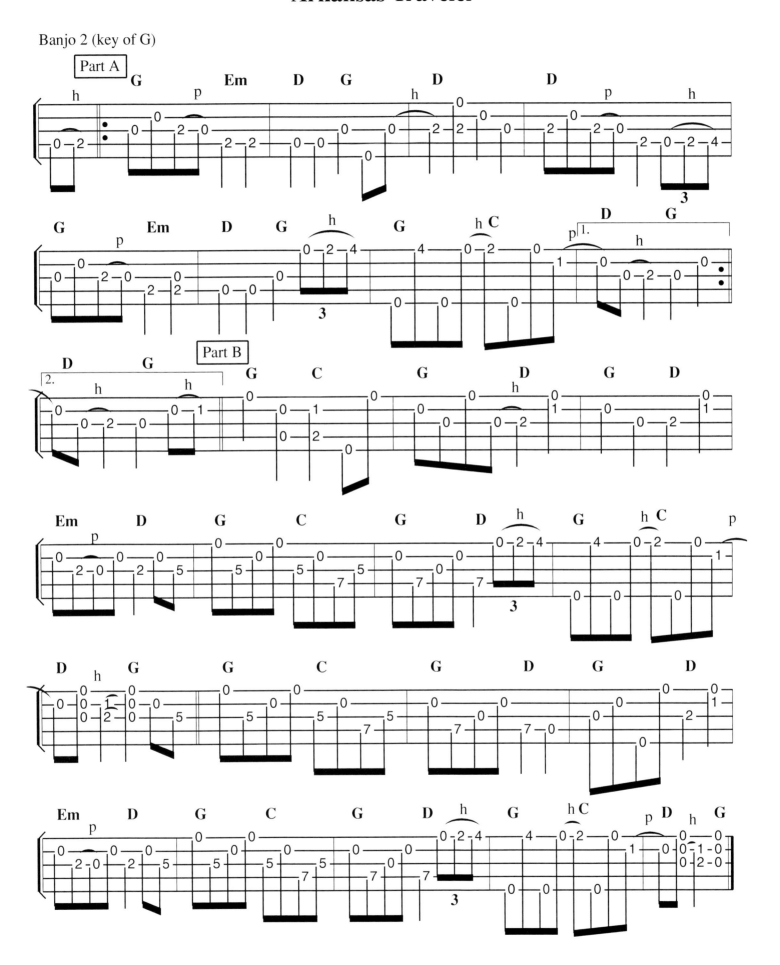

Arkansas Traveler

Banjo 3*

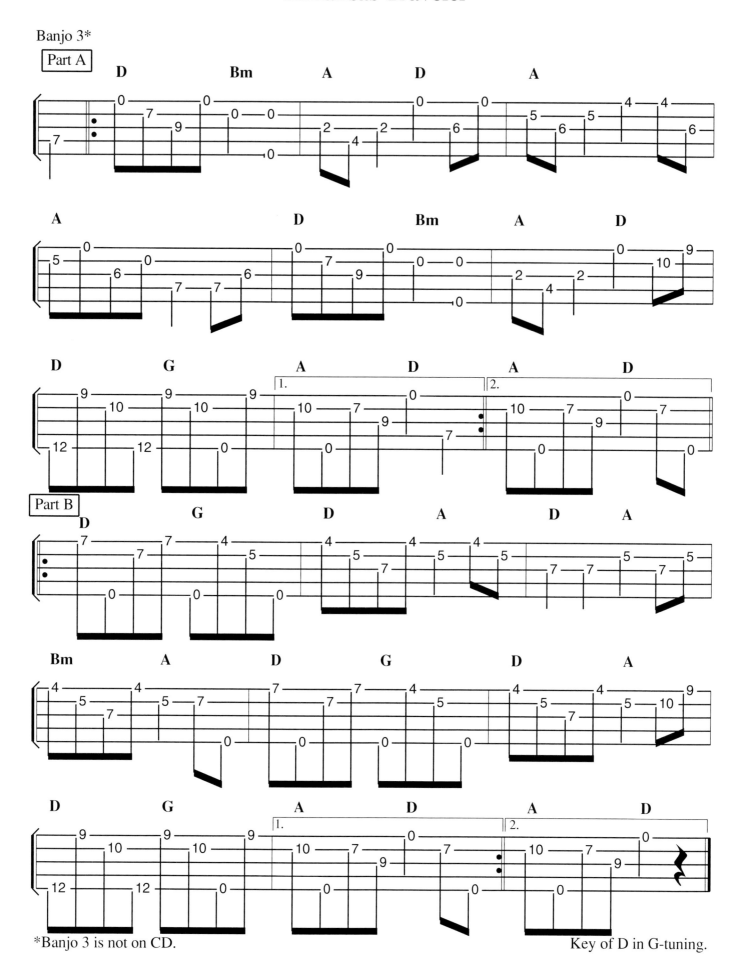

Key of D in G-tuning.

Arkansas Traveler

Banjo 4*

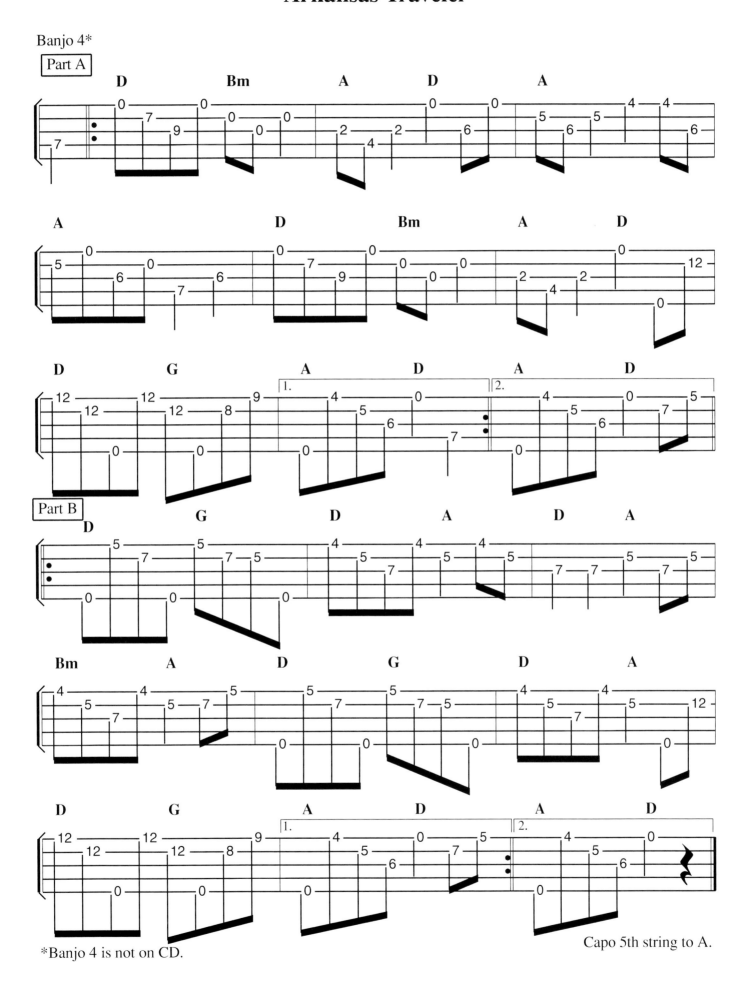

*Banjo 4 is not on CD.

Capo 5th string to A.

Aura Lee

Banjo 1 (capo 2)

Irish

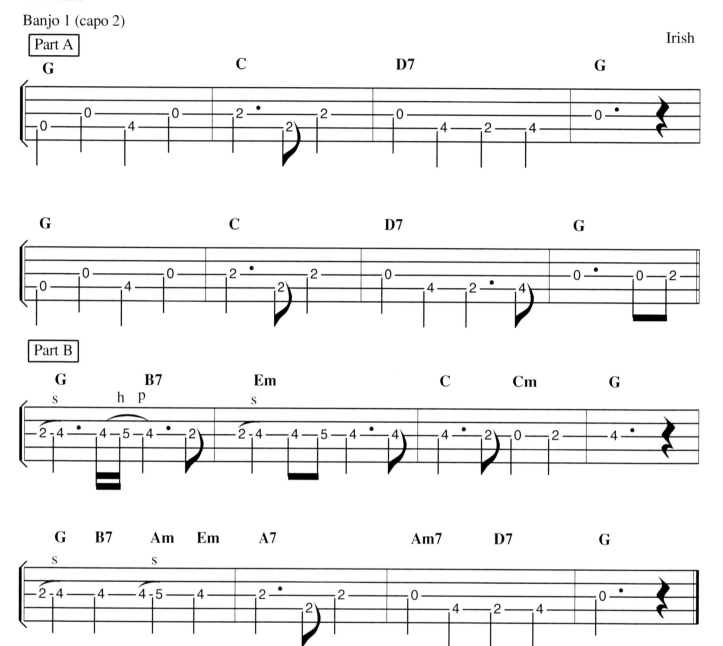

Aura Lee

Banjo 2*

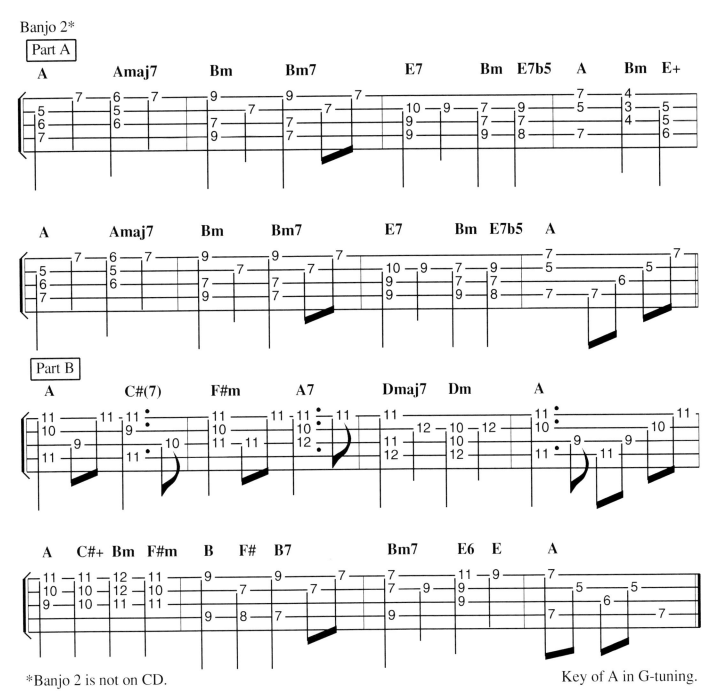

*Banjo 2 is not on CD.

Key of A in G-tuning.

This banjo part is in closed-chord position and can be shifted up or down to other keys.

The Battle Cry of Freedom

Banjo*

North American

*Banjo is not on CD.

Beaumont Rag

Banjo 1*

Part A

North American

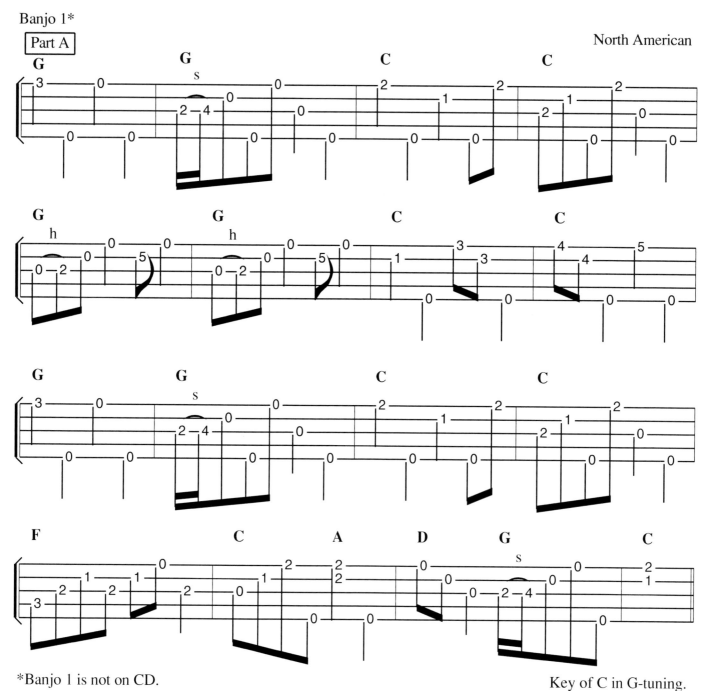

*Banjo 1 is not on CD.

Key of C in G-tuning.

Beaumont Rag

Banjo 1 (cont.)

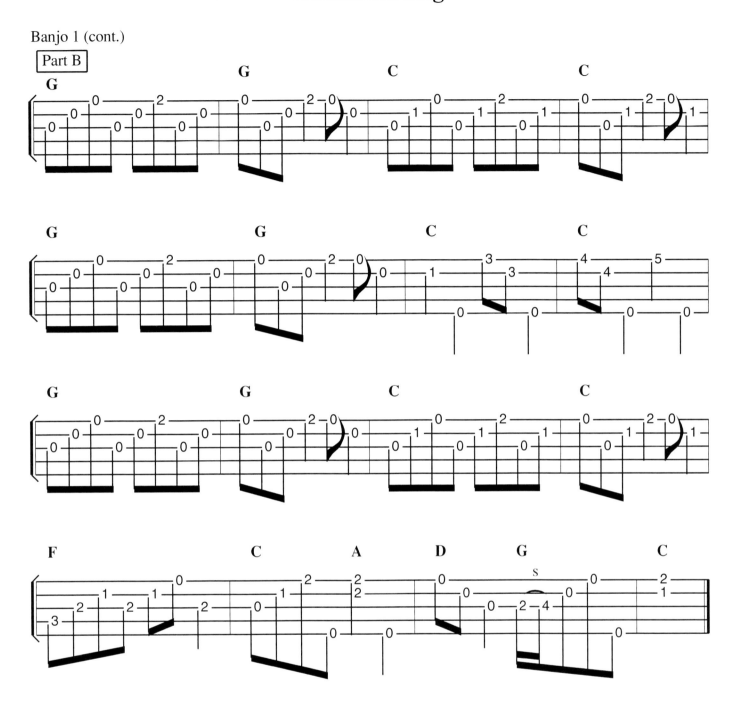

Beaumont Rag

Banjo 2*

Part A

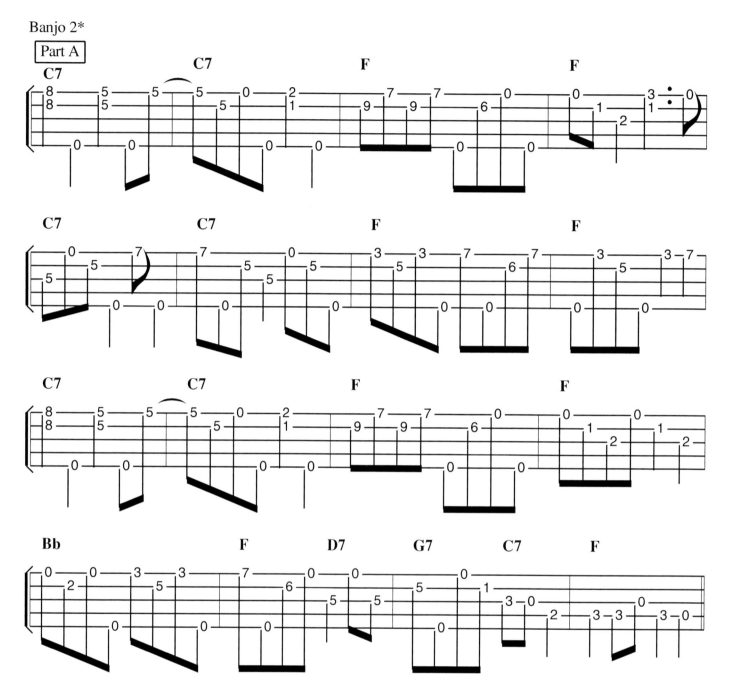

*Banjo 2 is not on CD.

20

Beaumont Rag

Banjo 2 (cont.)

Part B

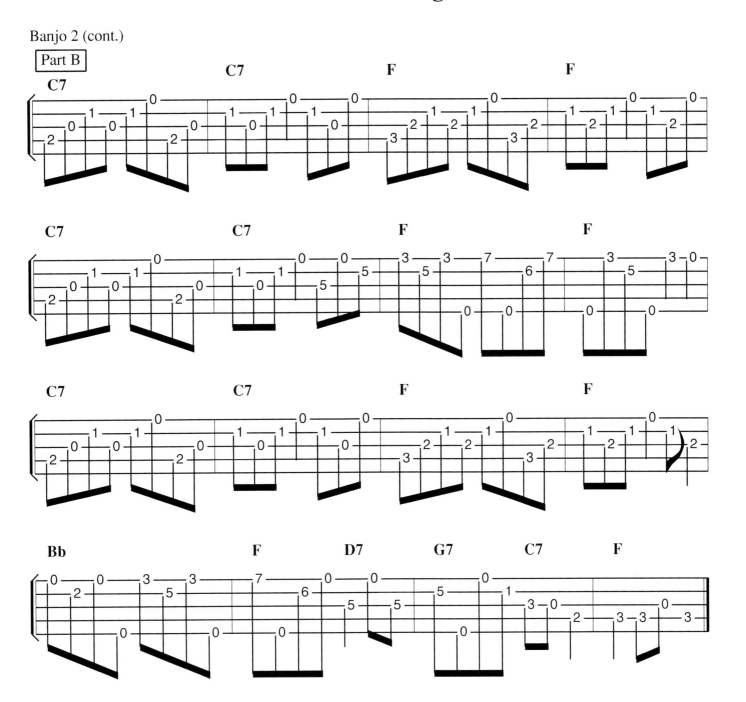

Billy in the Lowground

Banjo 1* (capo 5)

North American

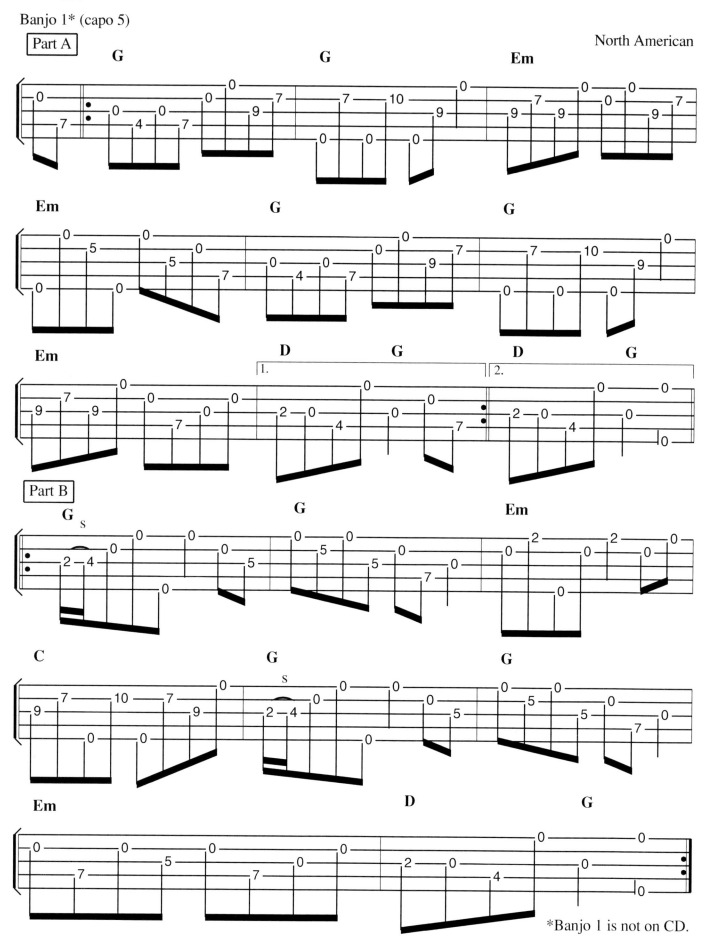

*Banjo 1 is not on CD.

Billy in the Lowground

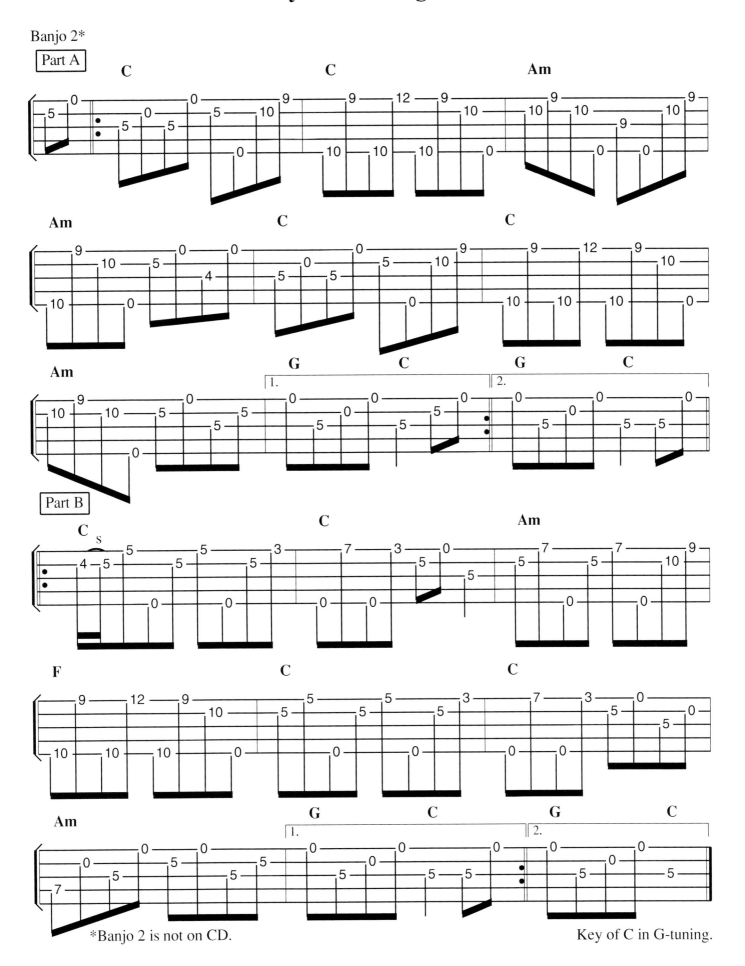

Banjo 2*

Part A

Part B

*Banjo 2 is not on CD.

Key of C in G-tuning.

23

Blackberry Blossom

Banjo 1

Part A

Australian

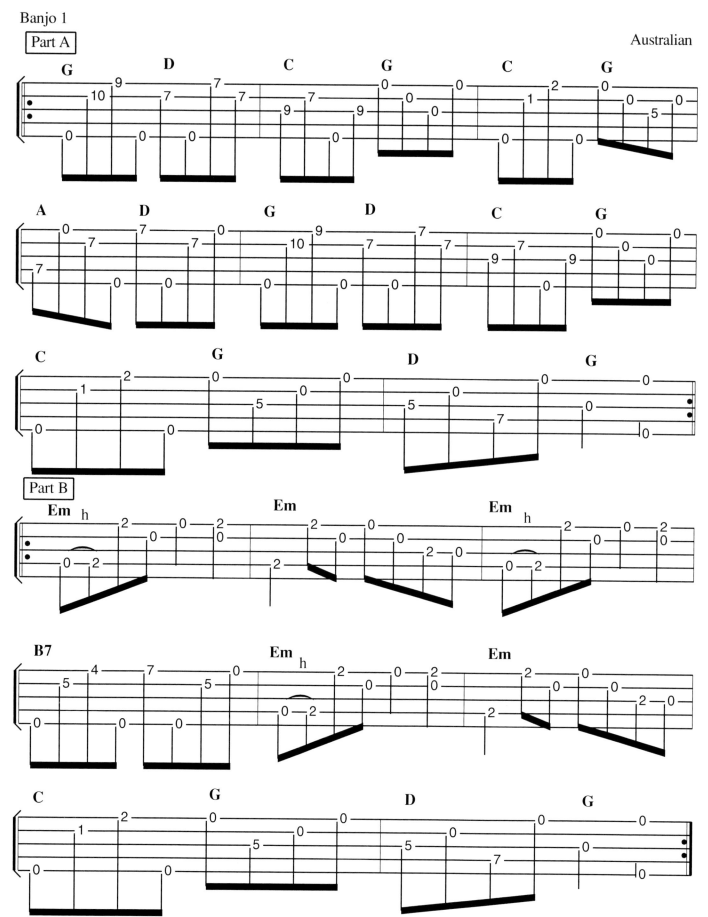

Blackberry Blossom

Banjo 2

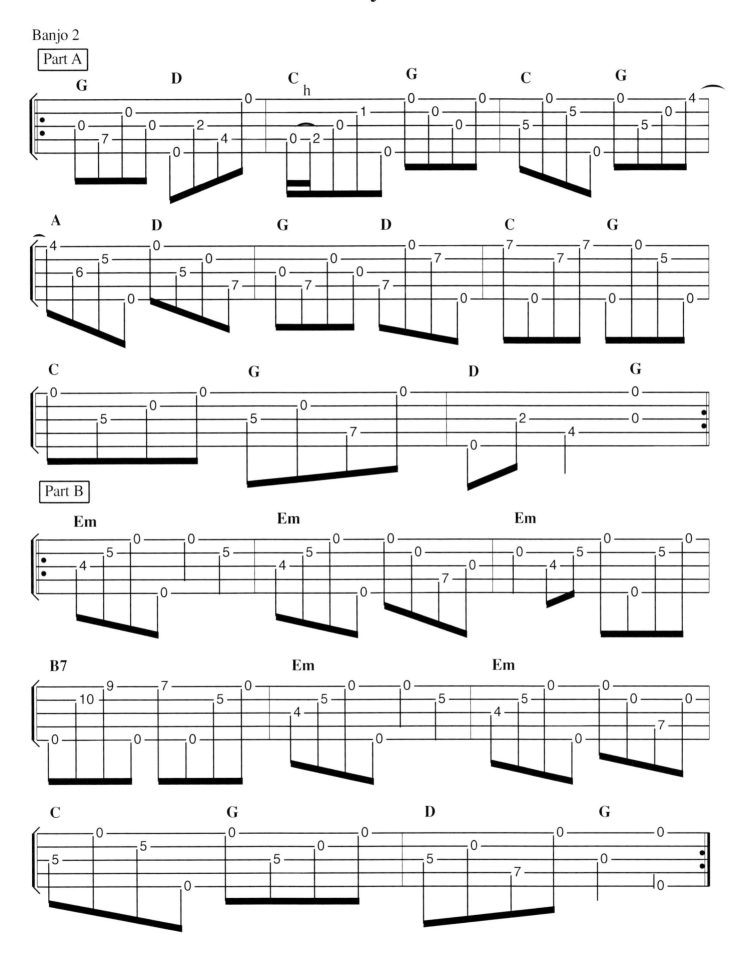

Bonaparte's Retreat

Banjo*

North American

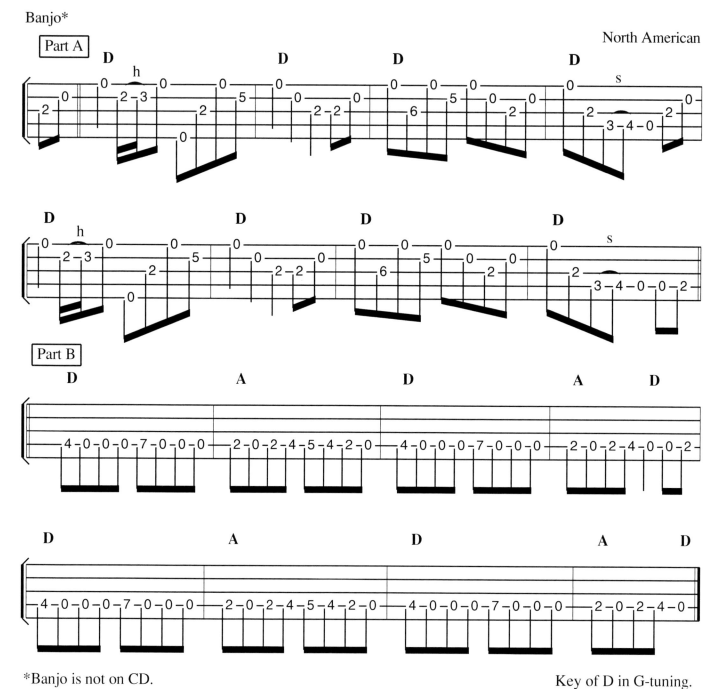

*Banjo is not on CD.

Key of D in G-tuning.
5th string may be capoed or tuned to 'A' or 'F♯'.

Carthage Waltz

Banjo

North American

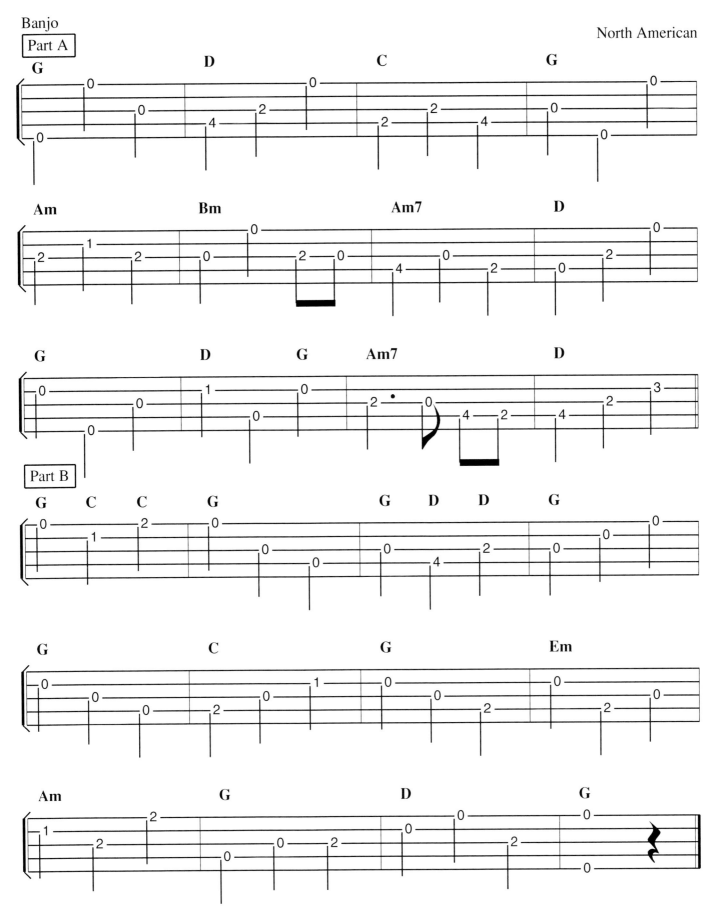

This page has been
left blank to avoid
awkward page turns.

Cherokee Shuffle

Banjo 1 (capo 2)

North American

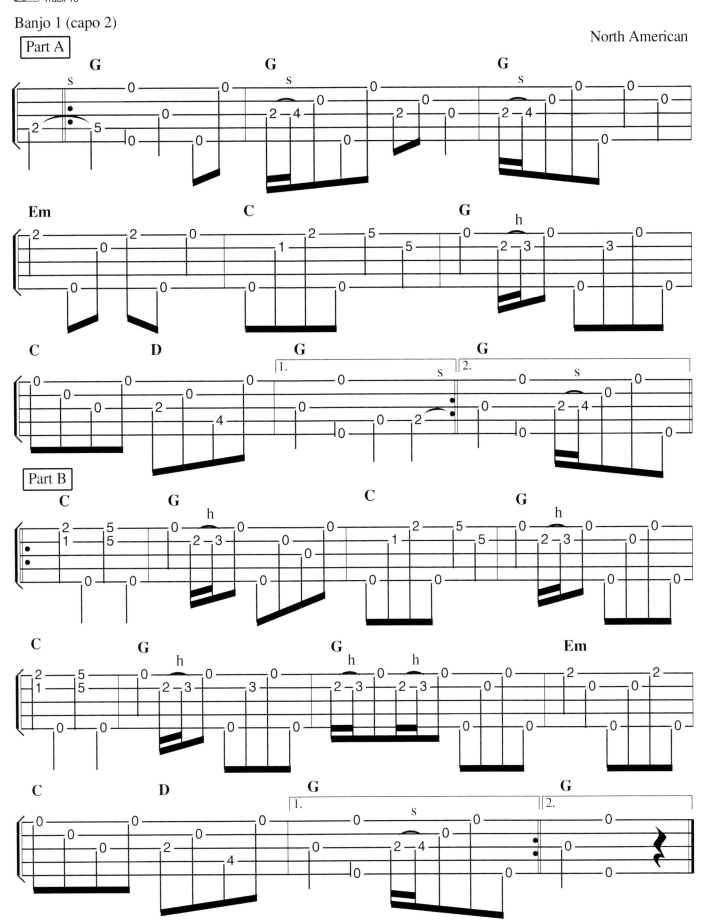

Cherokee Shuffle

Banjo 2*

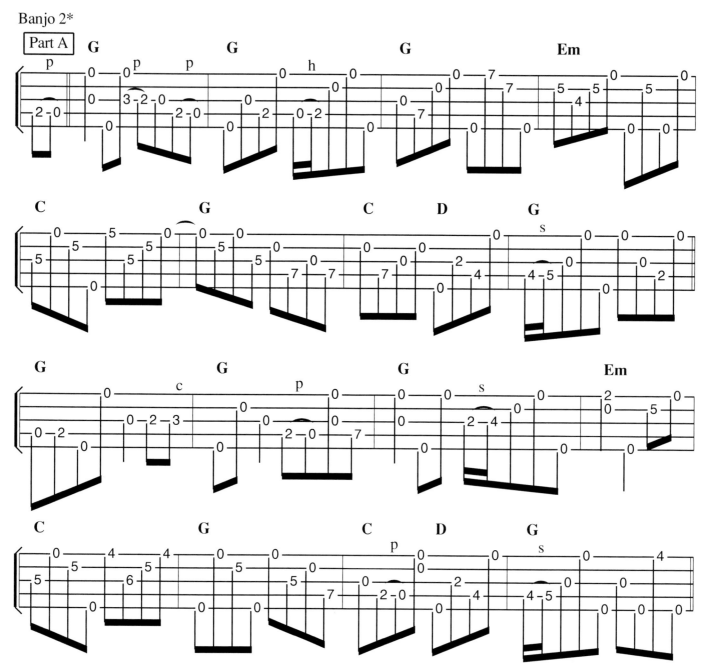

*Banjo 2 is not on CD.

Cherokee Shuffle

Banjo 2 (cont.)

Part B

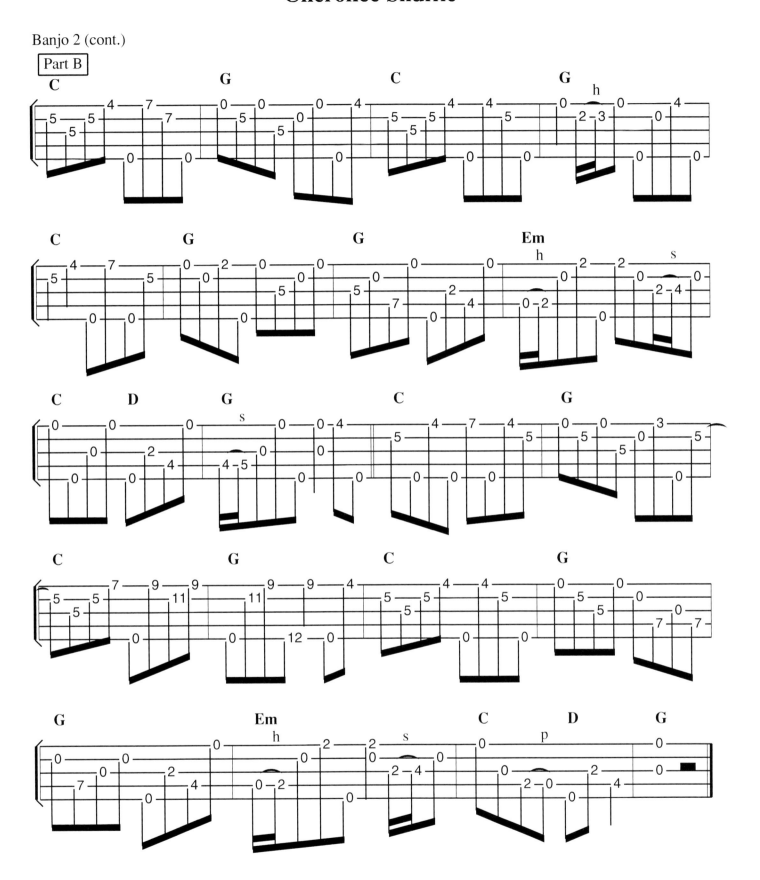

31

Cluck Old Hen

Banjo 1 (capo 2)

North American

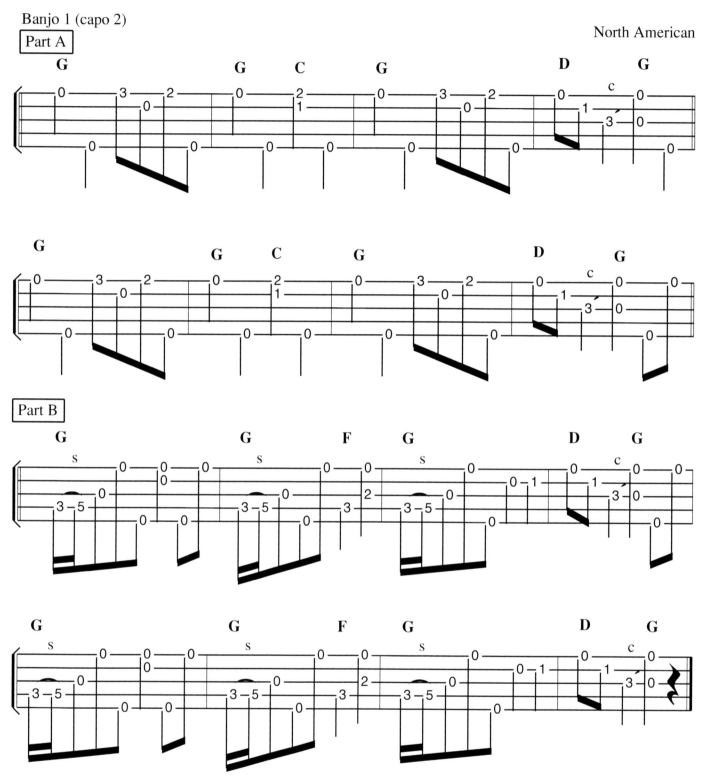

Cluck Old Hen

Banjo 2* (capo 2)

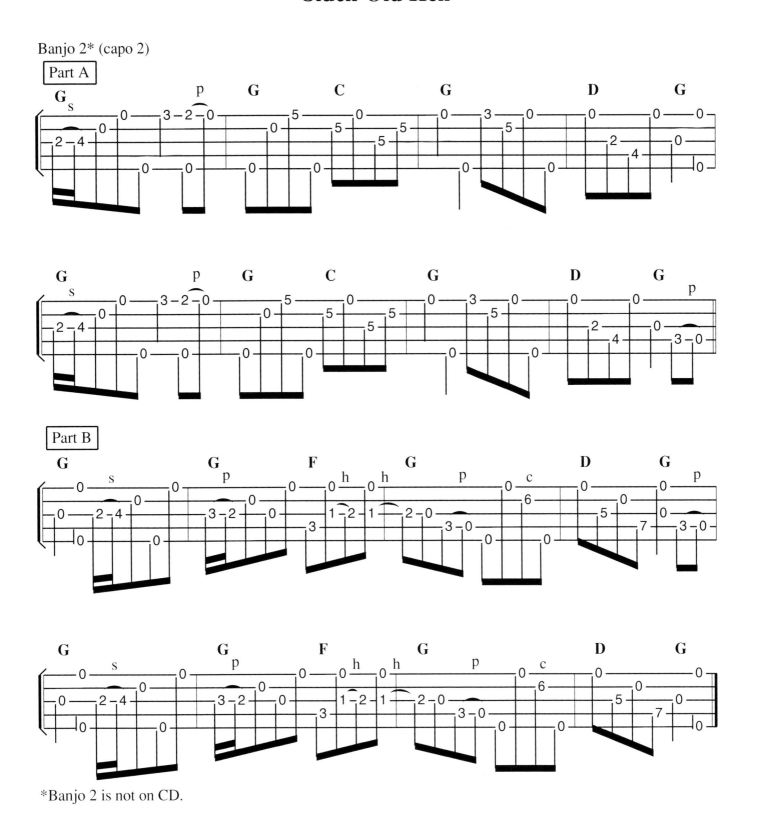

*Banjo 2 is not on CD.

Cotton-eyed Joe

Banjo 1* (capo 2)

North American

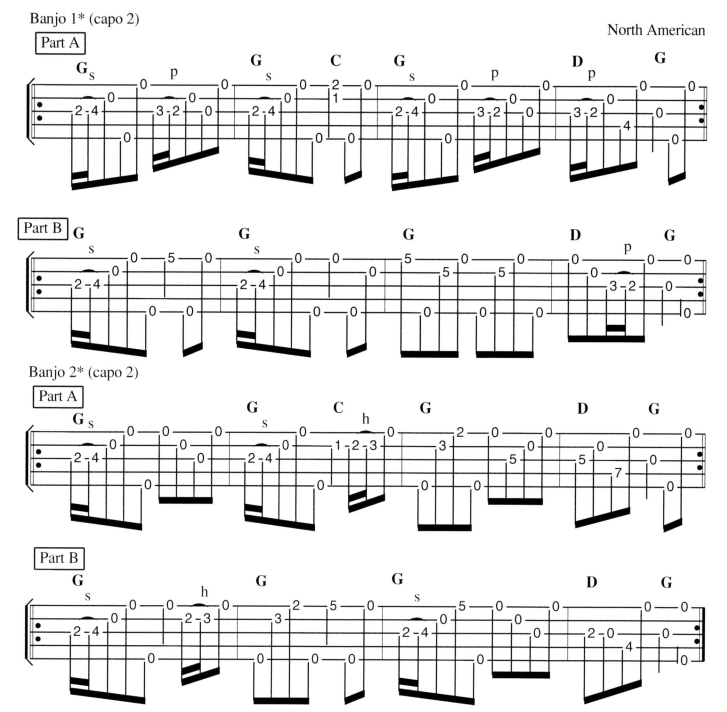

Banjo 2* (capo 2)

*Banjo 1 and 2 are not on CD.

Cotton Patch Rag

Banjo 1

North American

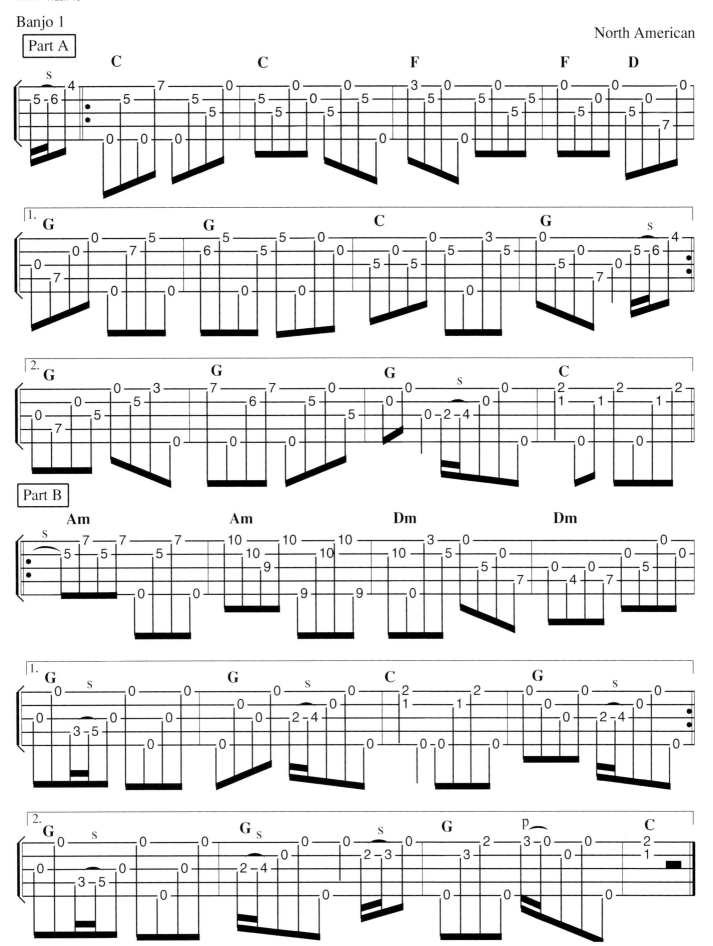

Cotton Patch Rag

Banjo 2*

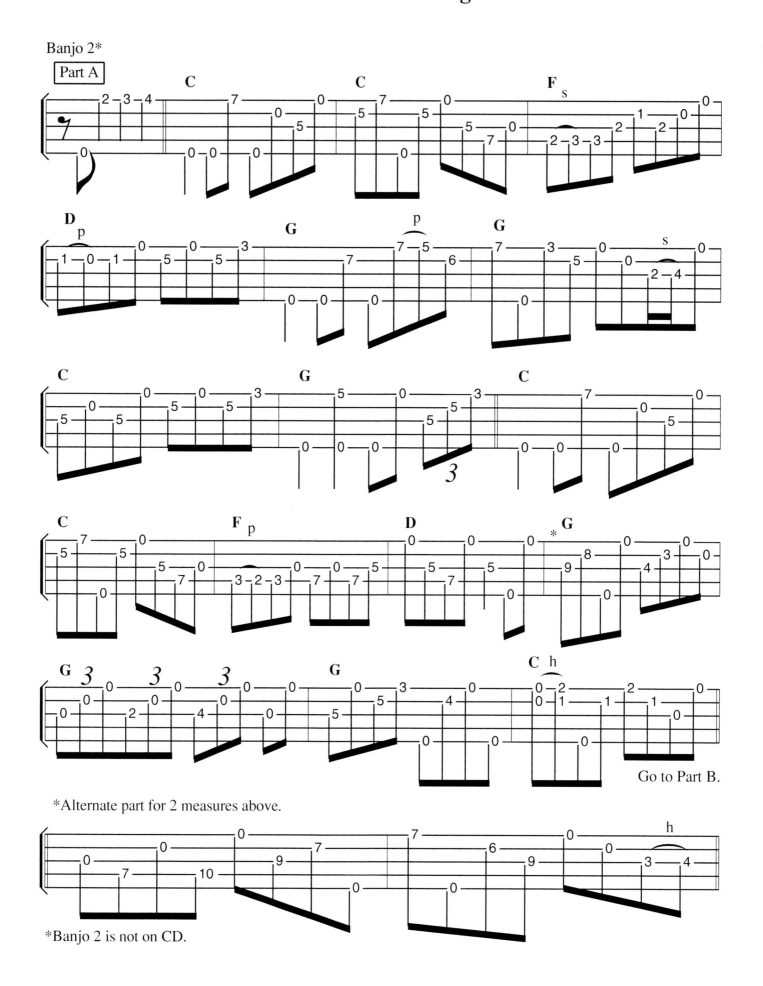

*Alternate part for 2 measures above.

Go to Part B.

*Banjo 2 is not on CD.

Cotton Patch Rag

Banjo 2 (cont.)

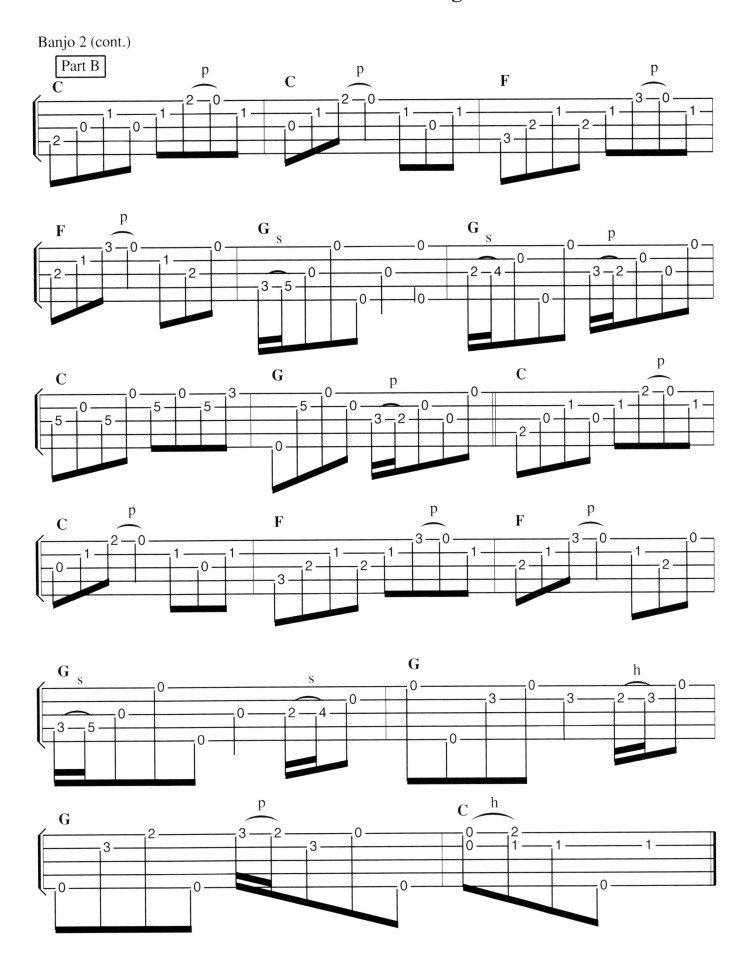

Cripple Creek

Banjo 1 (capo 2)

North American

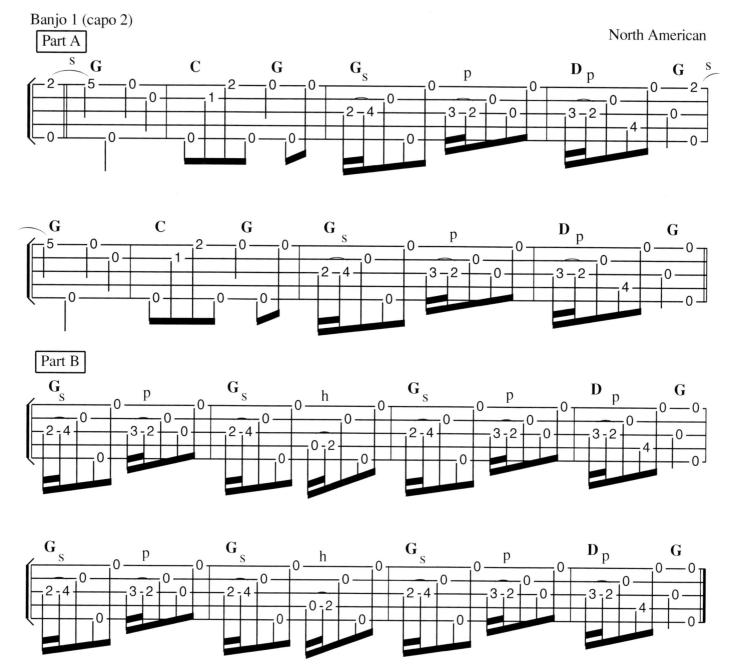

Cripple Creek

Banjo 2 (capo 2)

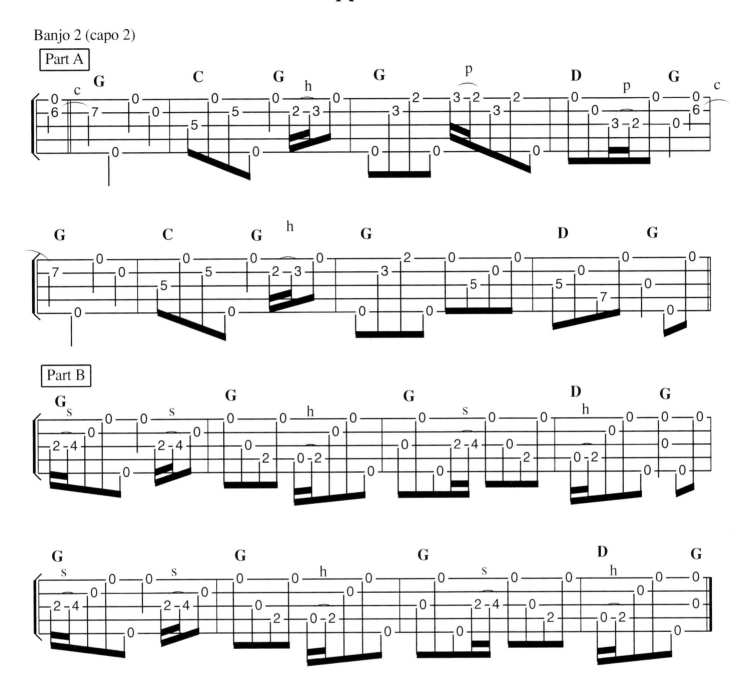

Cripple Creek

Banjo 3* (capo 2)

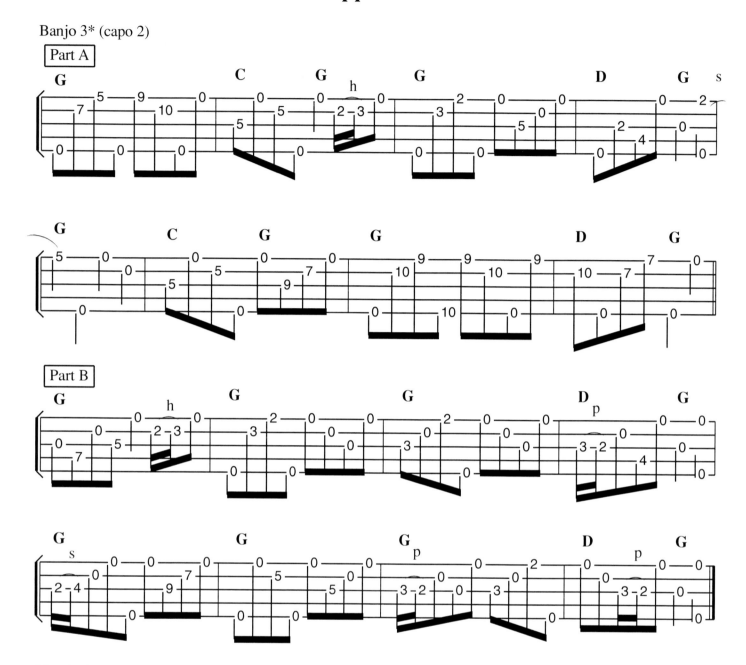

*Banjo 3 is not on CD.

Devil's Dream

Banjo (melody)* (capo 2)

North American

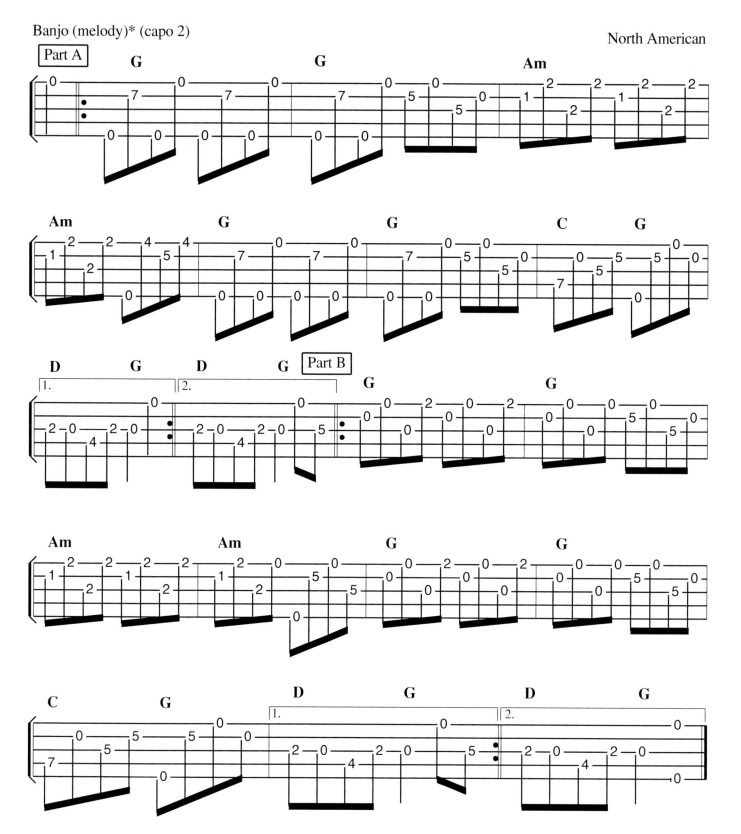

*Banjo melody is not on CD.

42

Devil's Dream

Banjo (high harmony)* (capo 2)

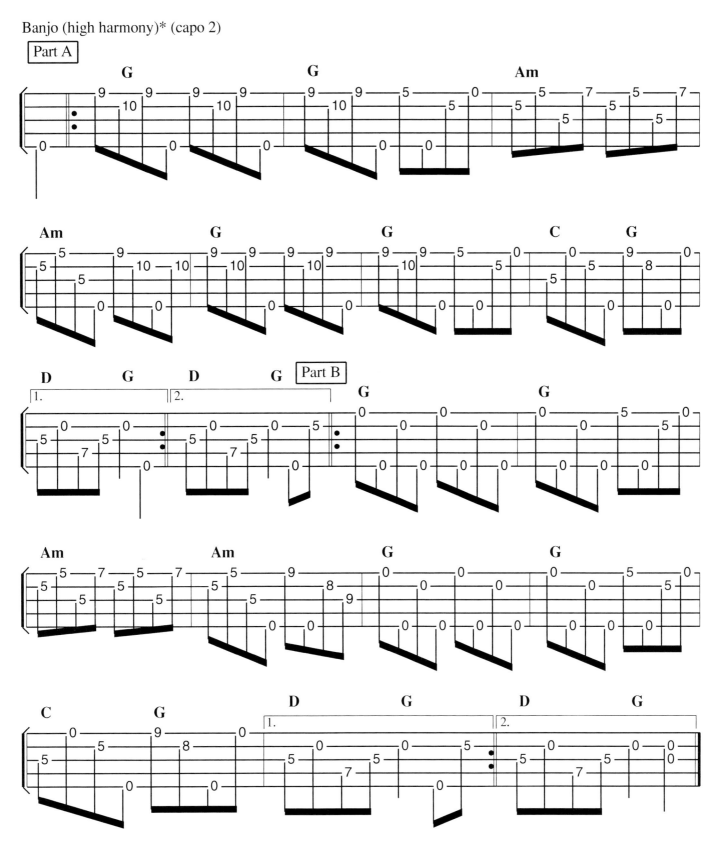

*Banjo high harmony is not on CD.

Devil's Dream

Banjo (low harmony)* (capo 2)

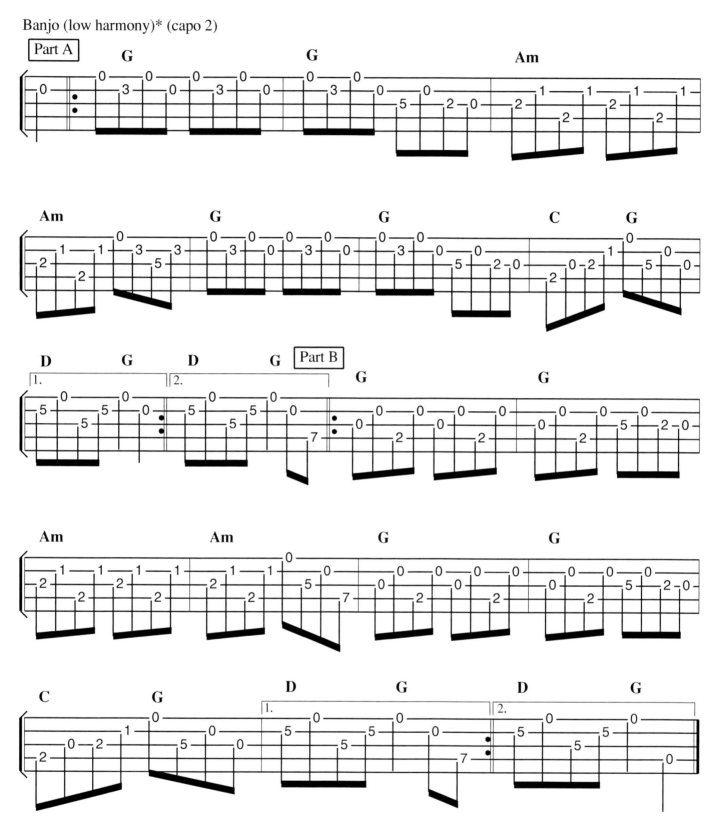

*Banjo low harmony is not on CD.

Down Yonder

Banjo

North American

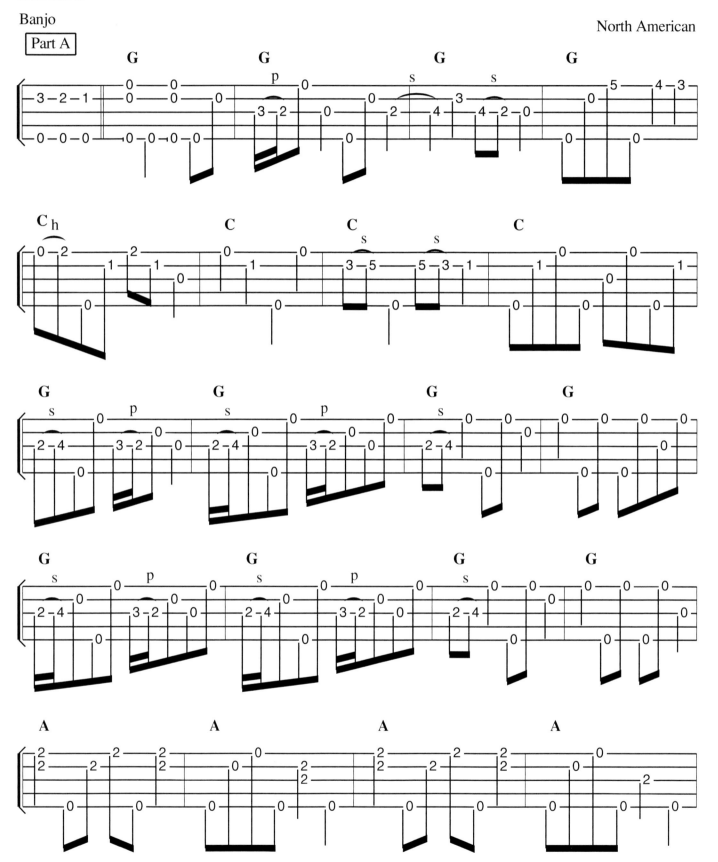

Down Yonder

Banjo (cont.)

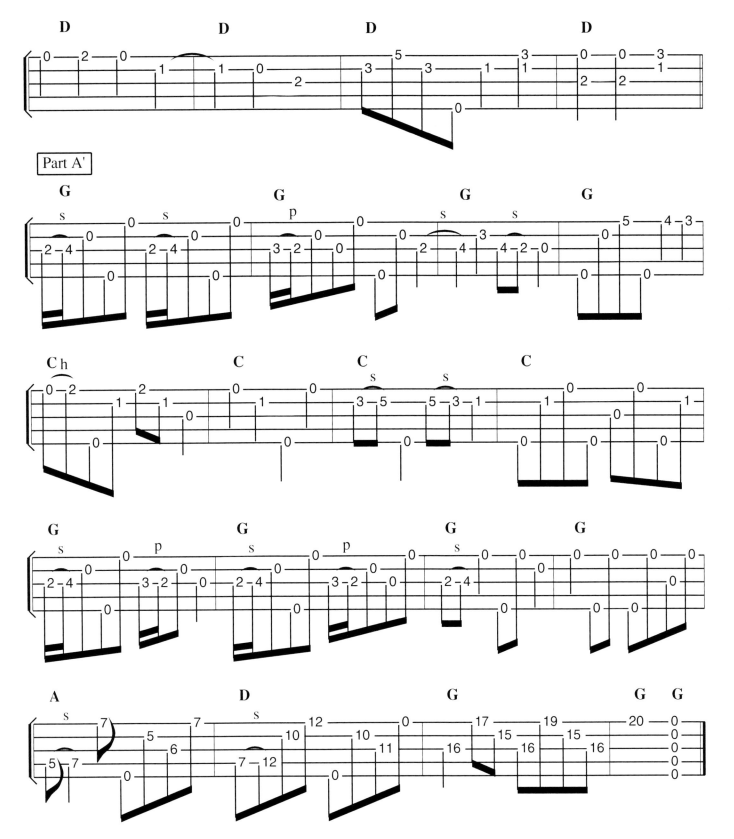

47

Eighth of January

Banjo 1*

North American

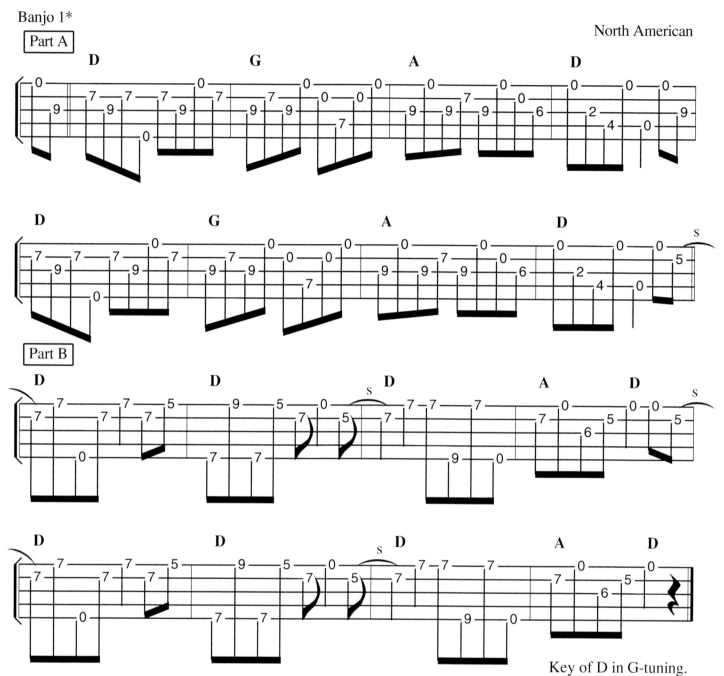

Key of D in G-tuning.

*Banjo 1 is not on CD.

Eighth of January

Banjo 2*

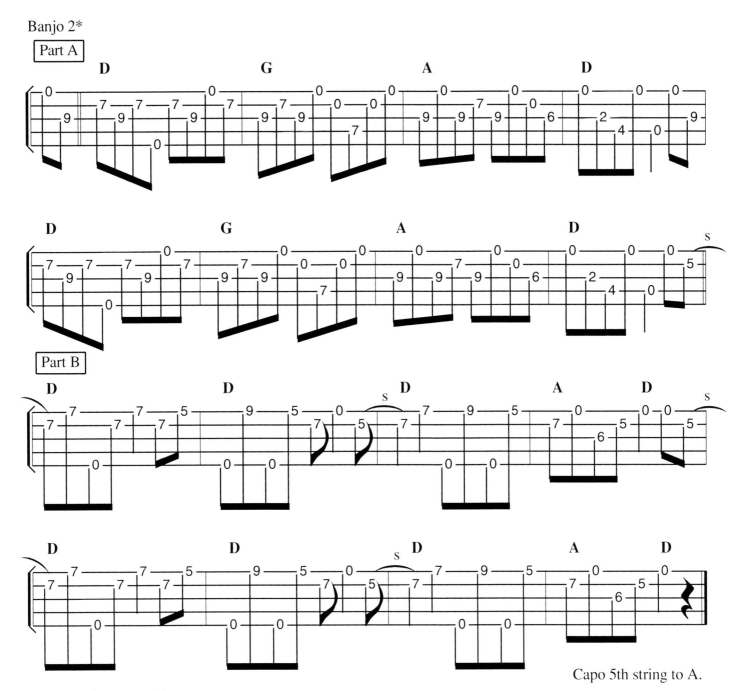

Capo 5th string to A.

*Banjo 2 is not on CD.

Forked Deer

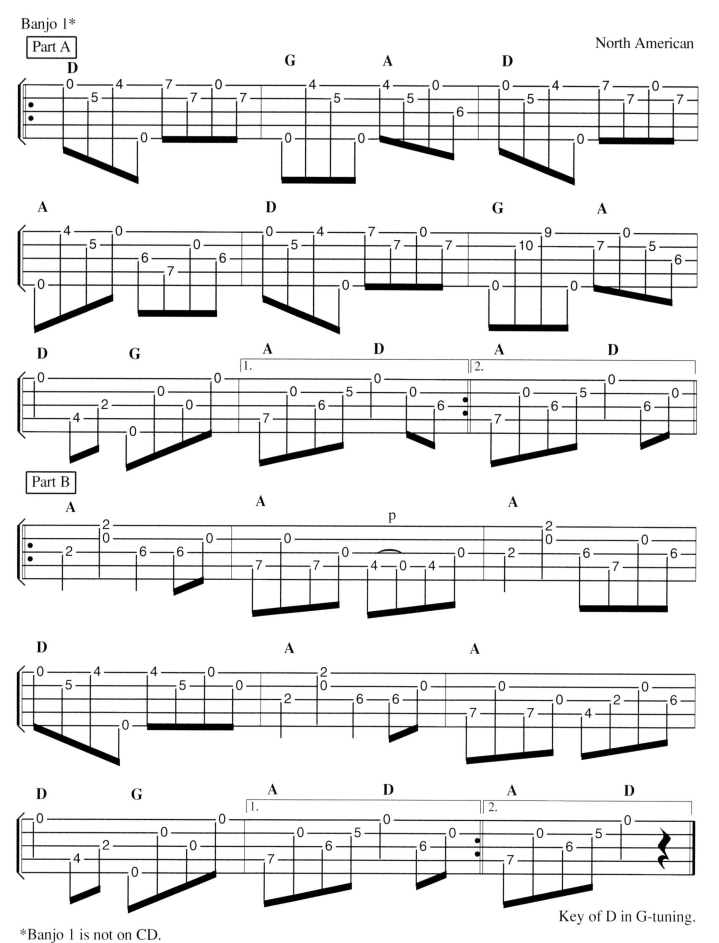

Banjo 1*

Part A

North American

Part B

Key of D in G-tuning.

*Banjo 1 is not on CD.

Forked Deer

Banjo 2* (capo 2)

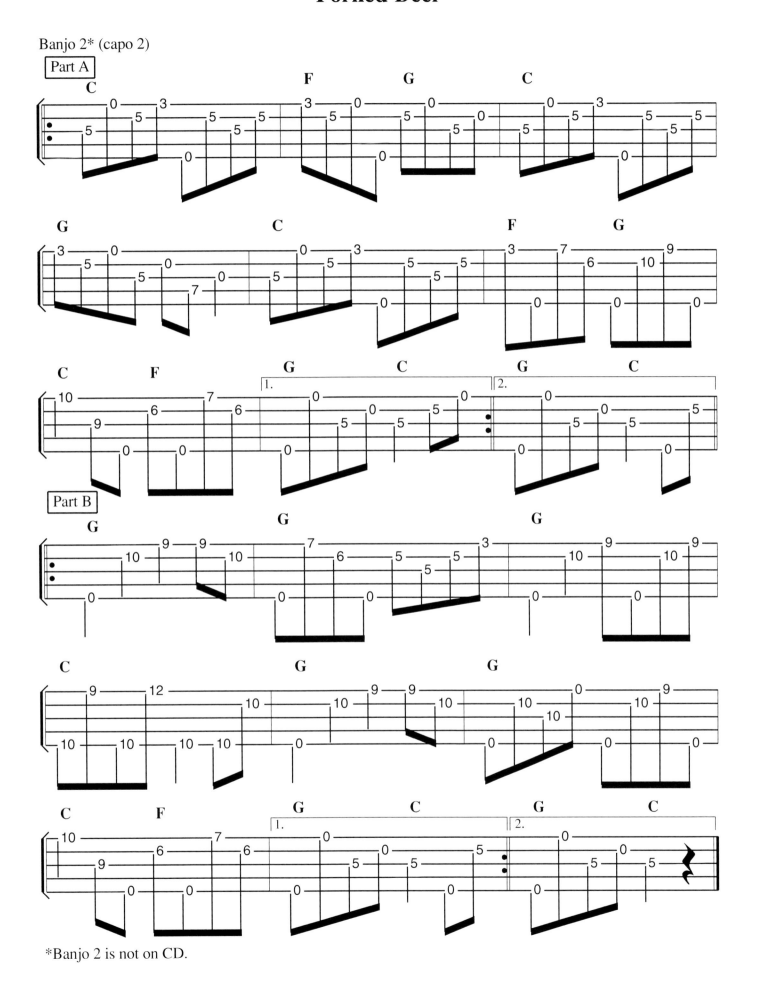

*Banjo 2 is not on CD.

Gardenia Waltz

Banjo*

North American

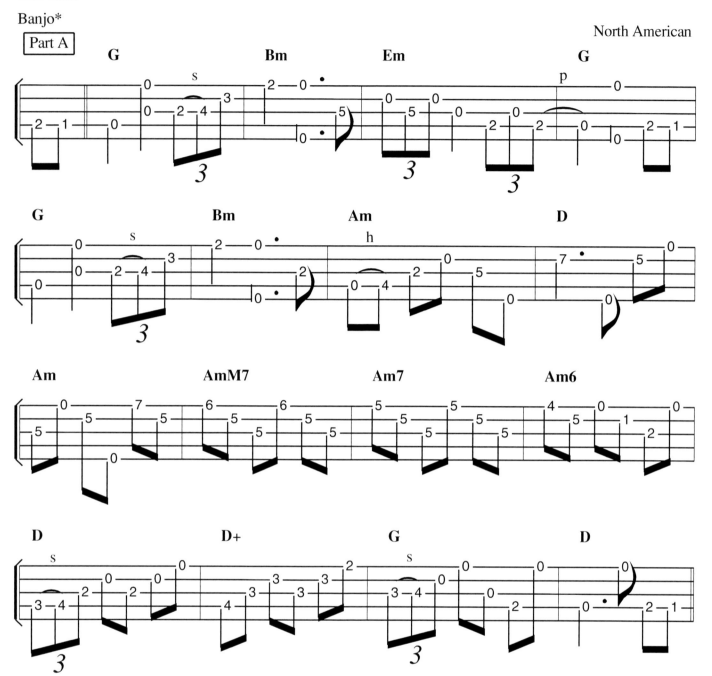

*Banjo is not on CD.

Gardenia Waltz

Banjo (cont.)

Part B

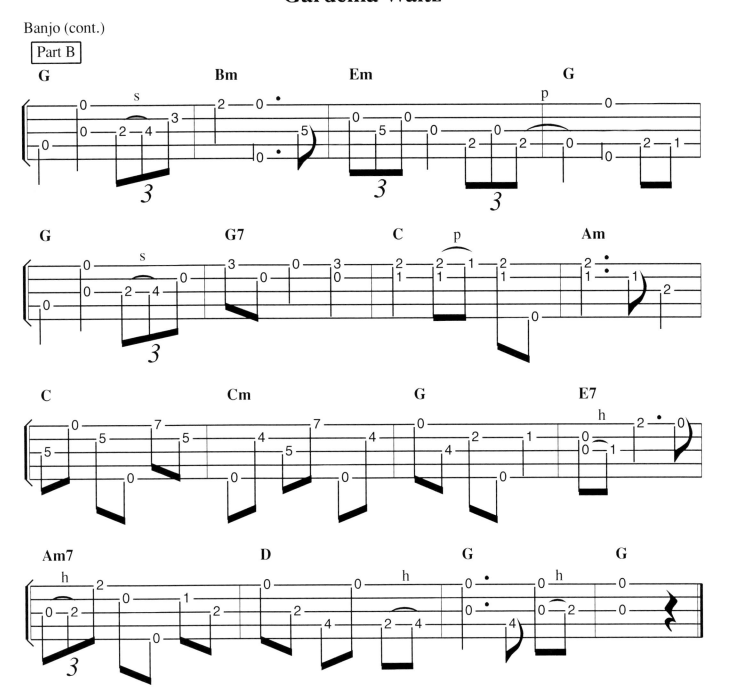

Grandfather's Clock

Banjo 1*

North American

Part A

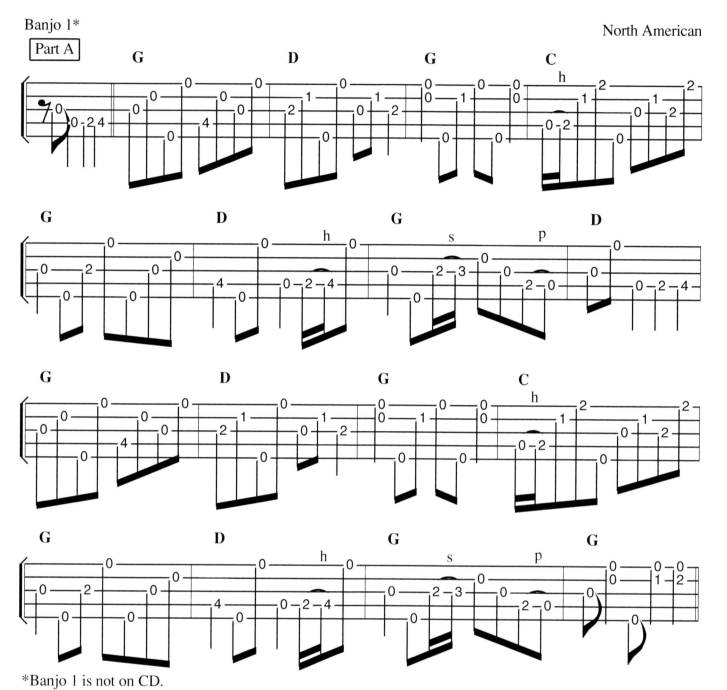

*Banjo 1 is not on CD.

Grandfather's Clock

Banjo 1 (cont.)

Part B

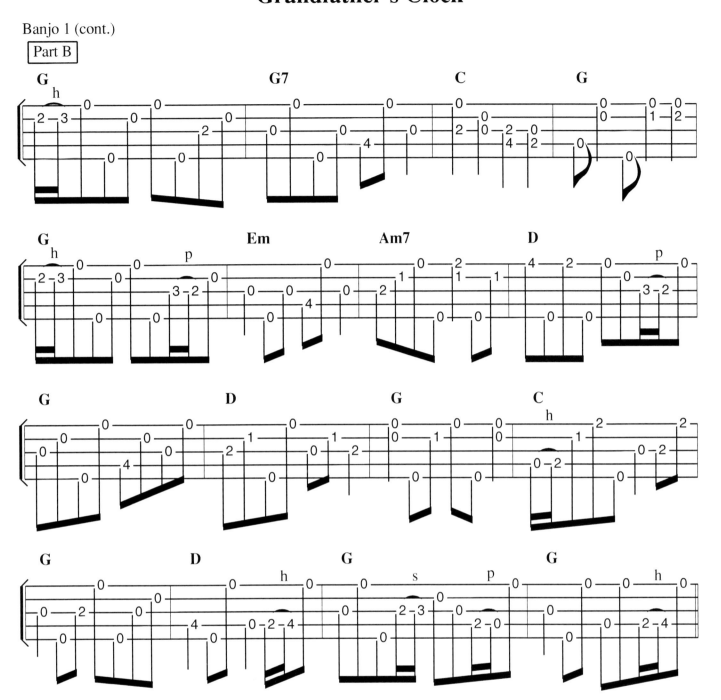

Grandfather's Clock

Banjo 1 (cont.)

Part C

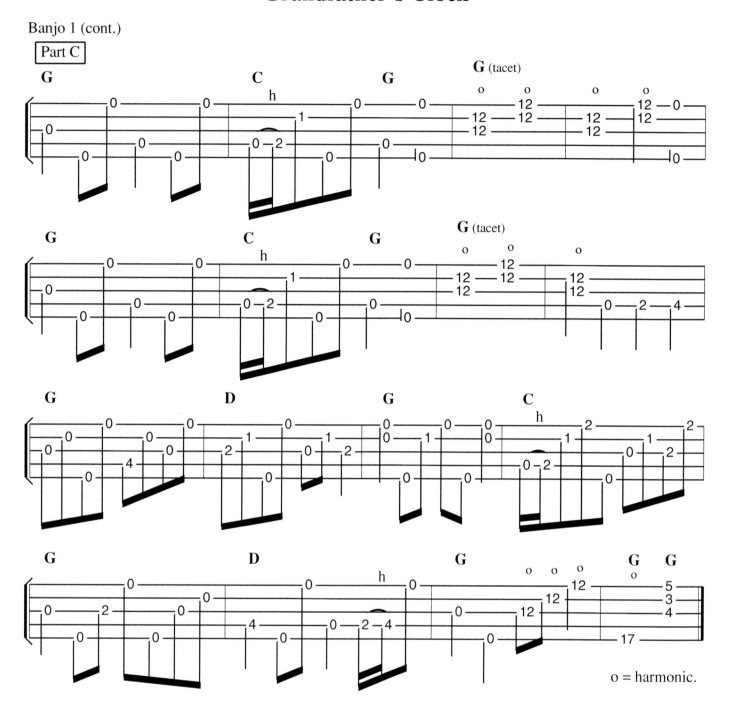

o = harmonic.

Grandfather's Clock

Banjo 2

Part A

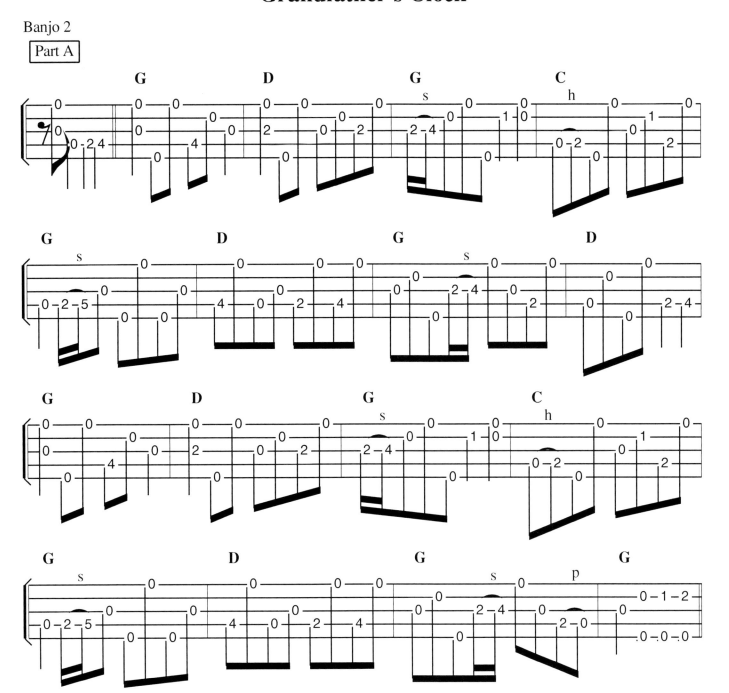

Grandfather's Clock

Banjo 2 (cont.)

Part B

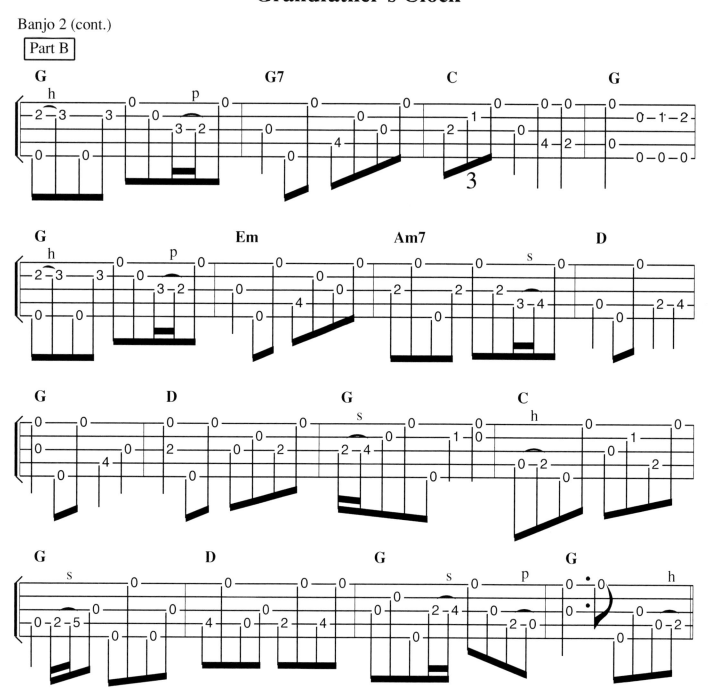

Grandfather's Clock

Banjo 2 (cont.)

Part C

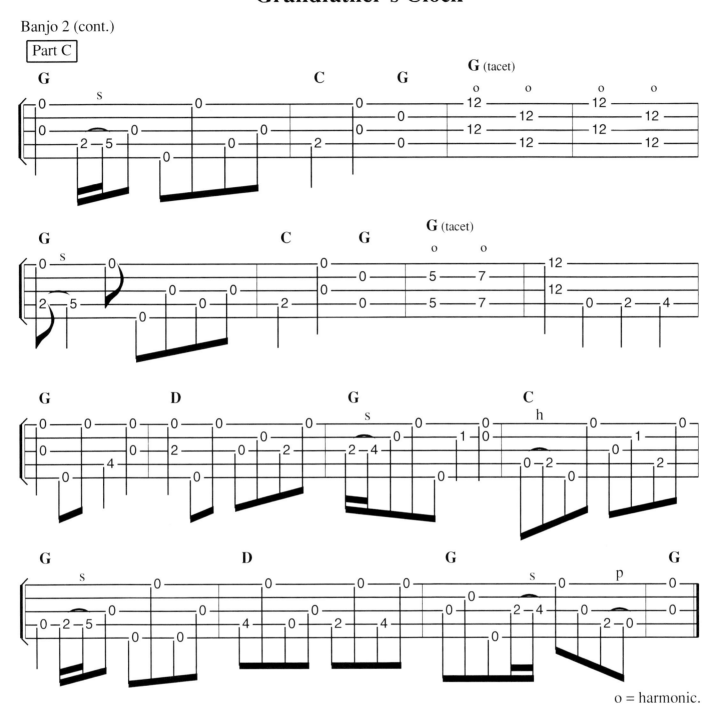

o = harmonic.

Green Willis

Banjo 1 (capo 7)

Irish/American

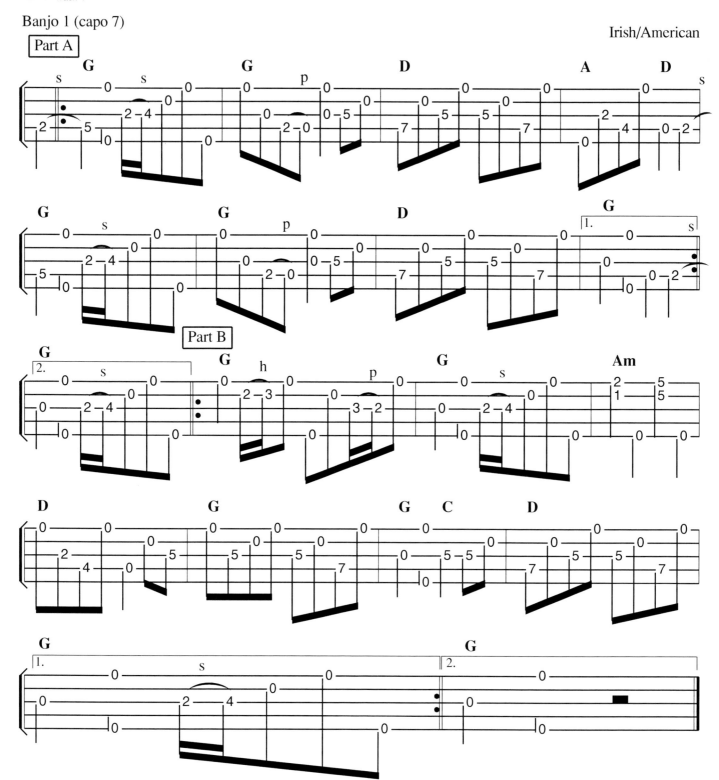

Green Willis

Banjo 2*

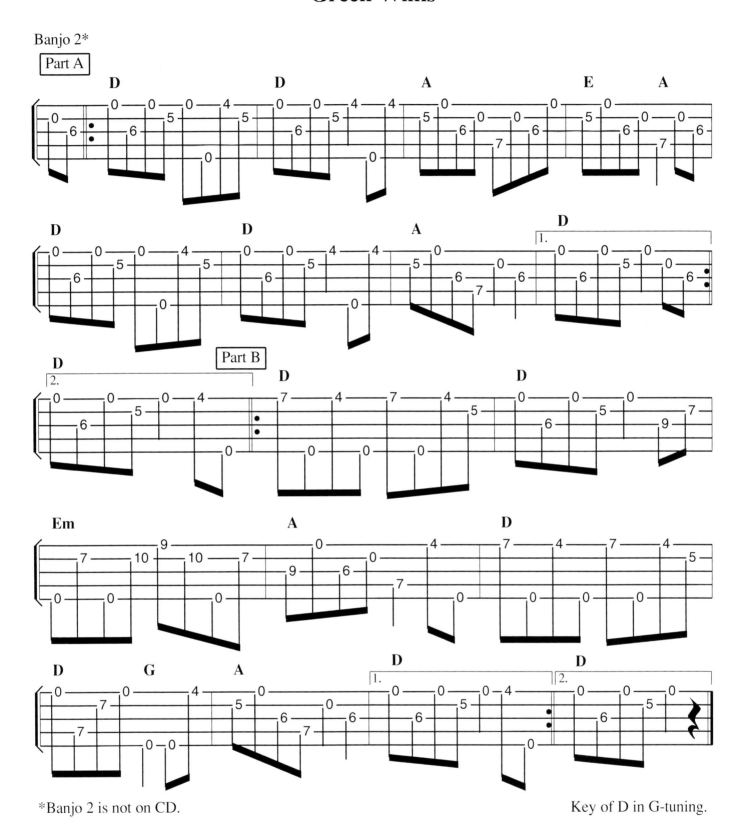

*Banjo 2 is not on CD.

Key of D in G-tuning.

Green Willis

Banjo 3*

Part A

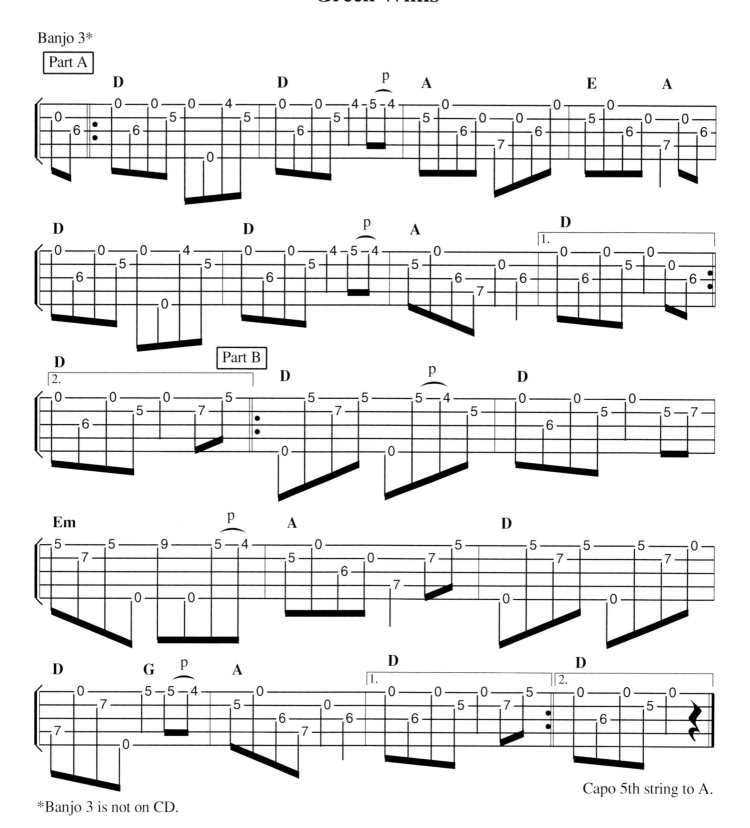

Capo 5th string to A.

*Banjo 3 is not on CD.

Indian's Farewell Waltz

Banjo* (capo 2)*

North America

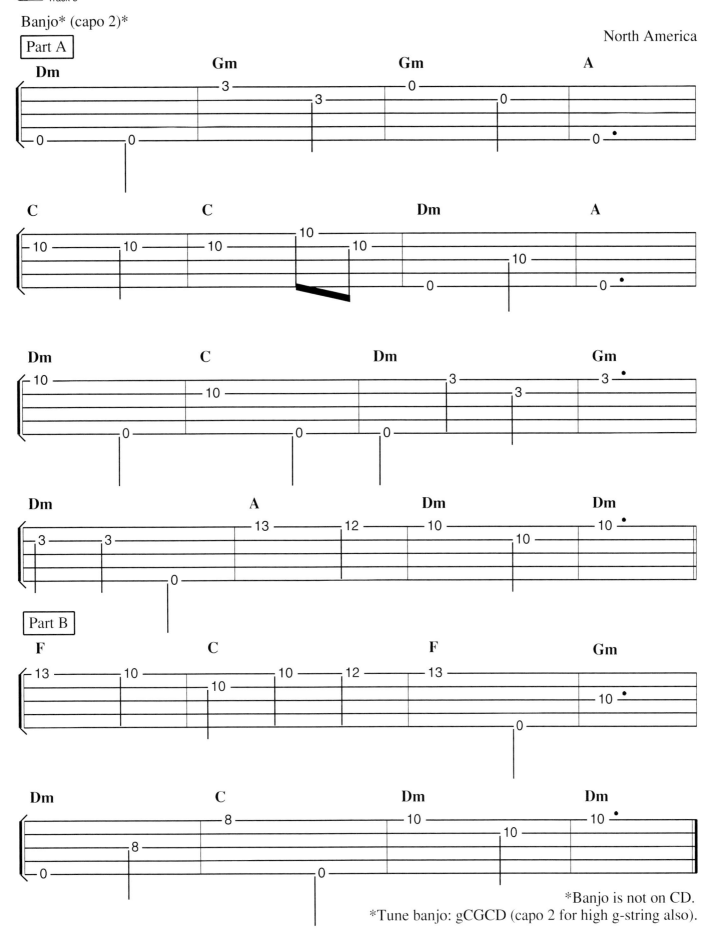

*Banjo is not on CD.
*Tune banjo: gCGCD (capo 2 for high g-string also).

*This page has been
left blank to avoid
awkward page turns.*

Irish Washerwoman

Banjo*

Part A

Irish

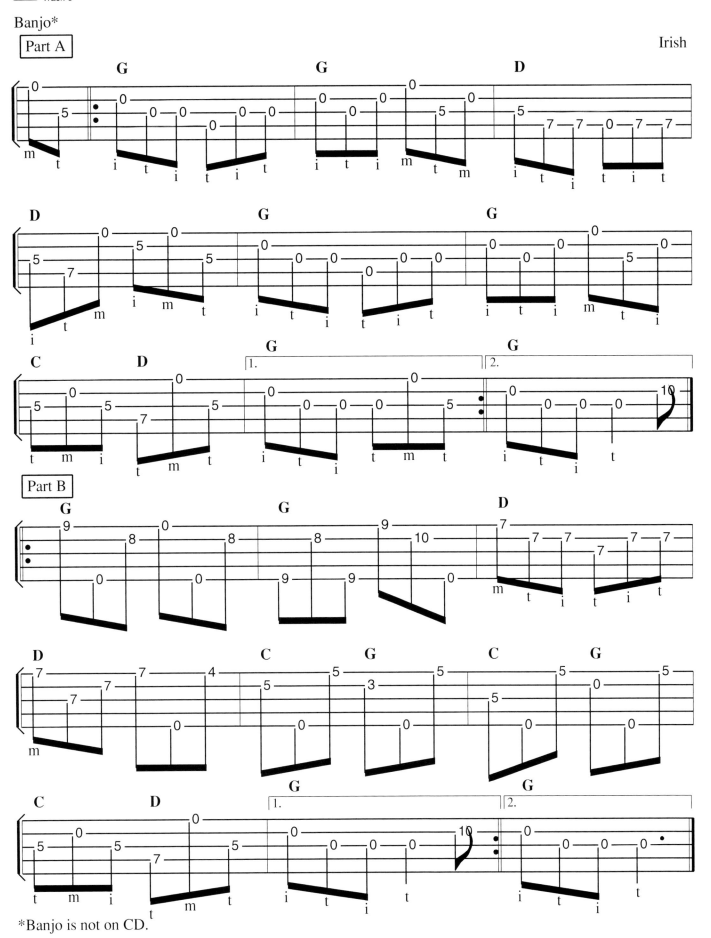

Part B

*Banjo is not on CD.

La Bastringue

Banjo*

French Canadian

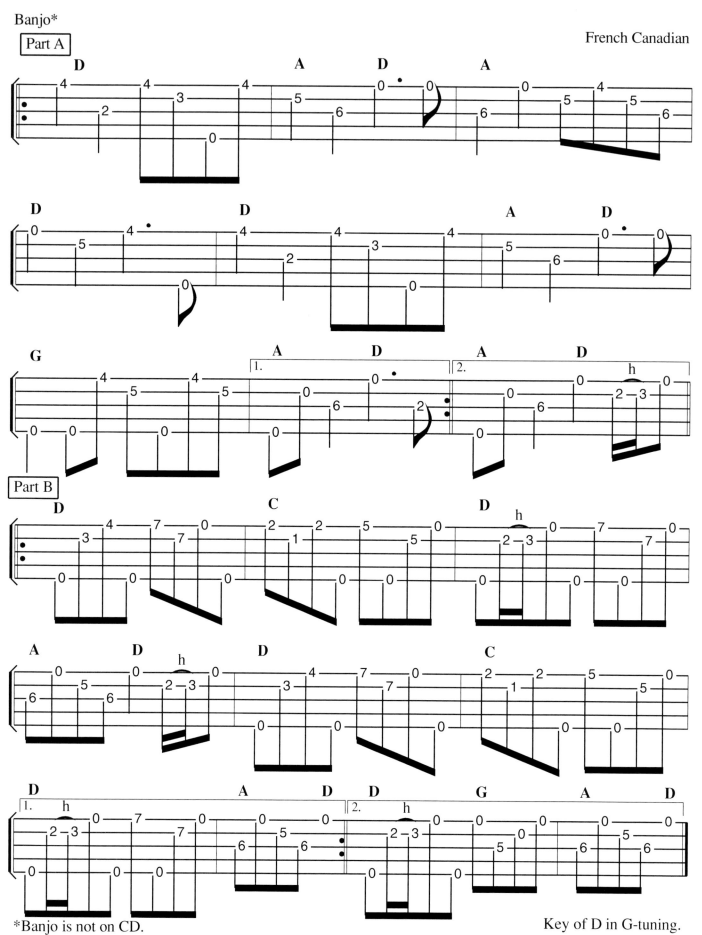

*Banjo is not on CD.

Key of D in G-tuning.

Leather Britches

Banjo*

North American

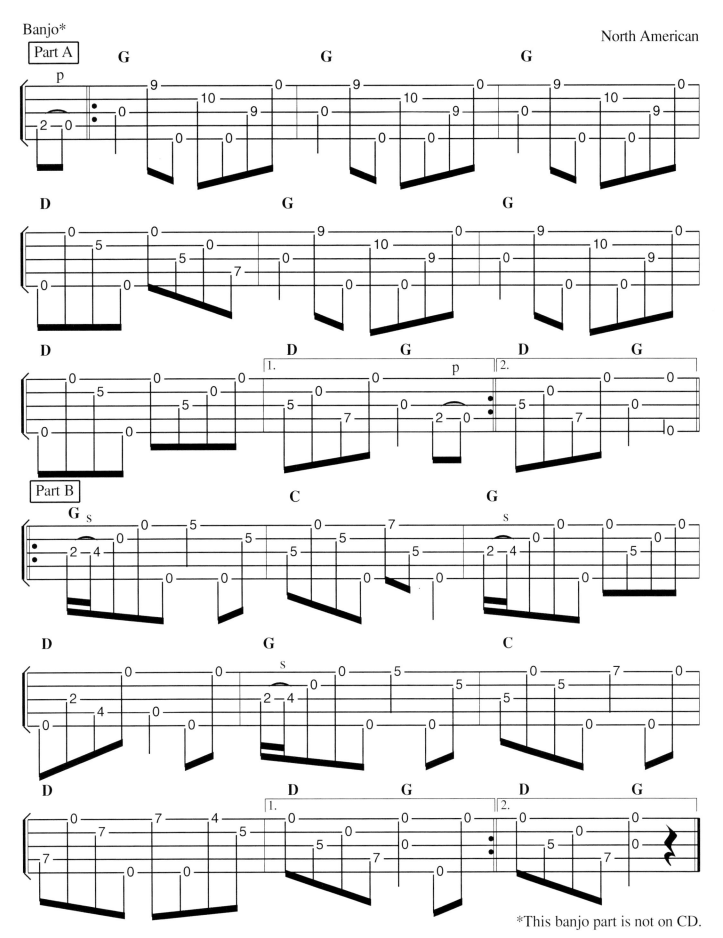

*This banjo part is not on CD.

Liberty

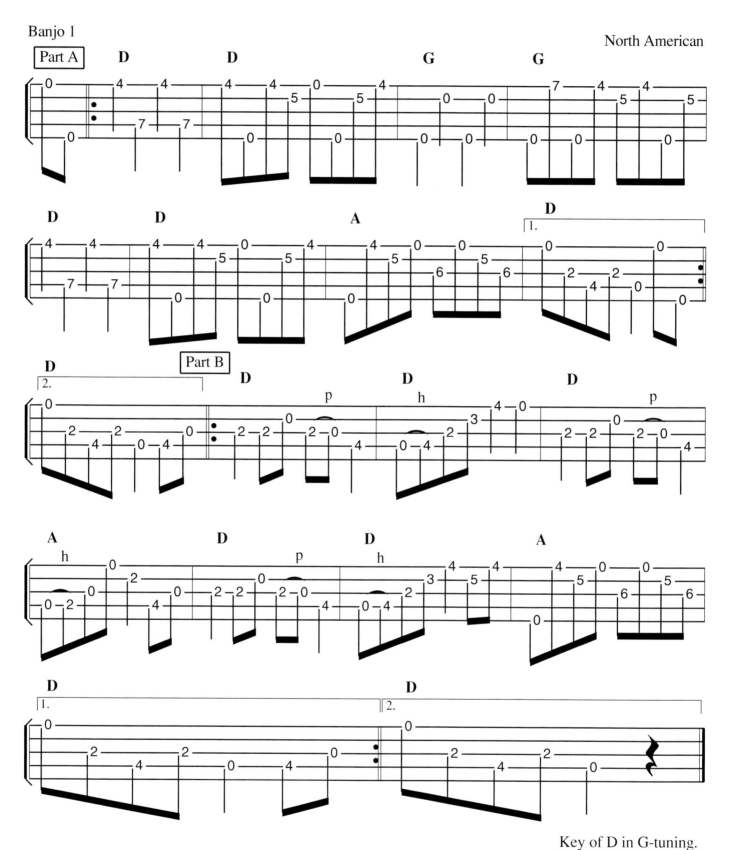

Key of D in G-tuning.

Liberty

Banjo 1* (alt. B-part)

Part B

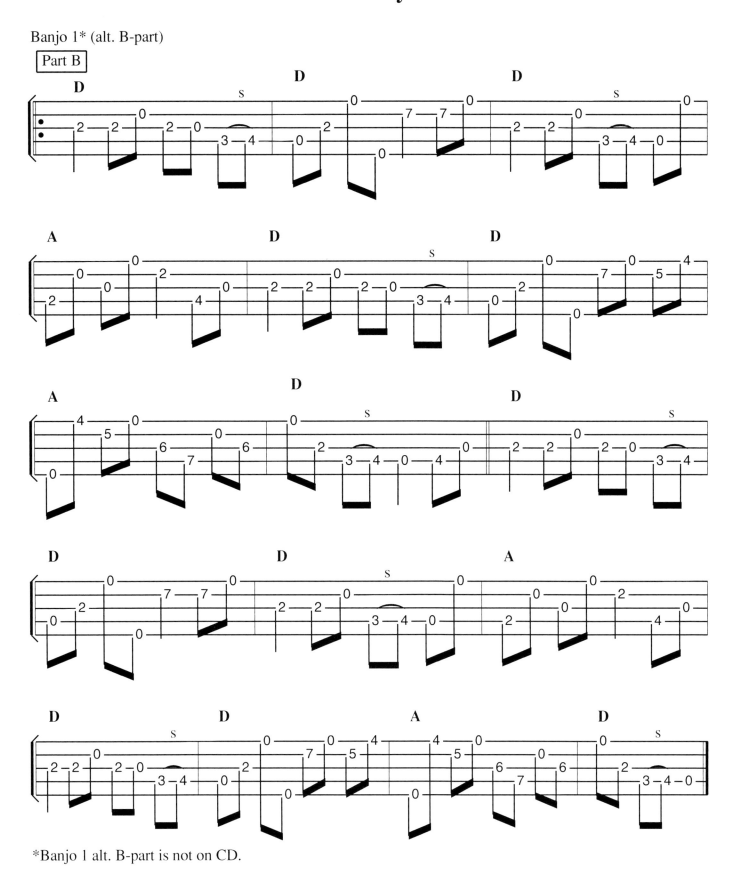

*Banjo 1 alt. B-part is not on CD.

Liberty

Banjo 2* (capo 2)

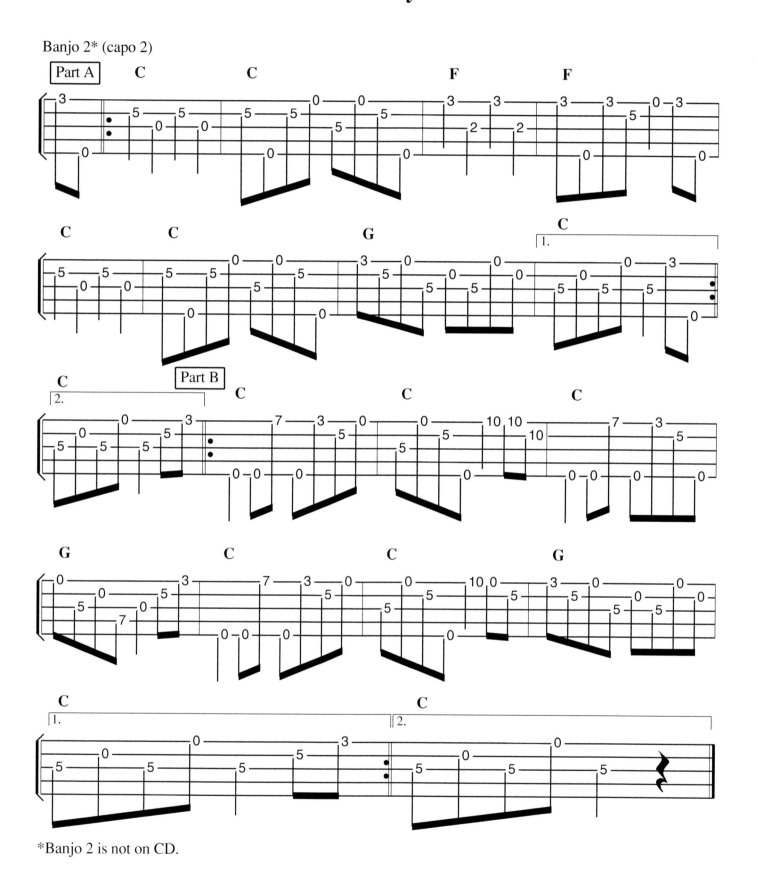

*Banjo 2 is not on CD.

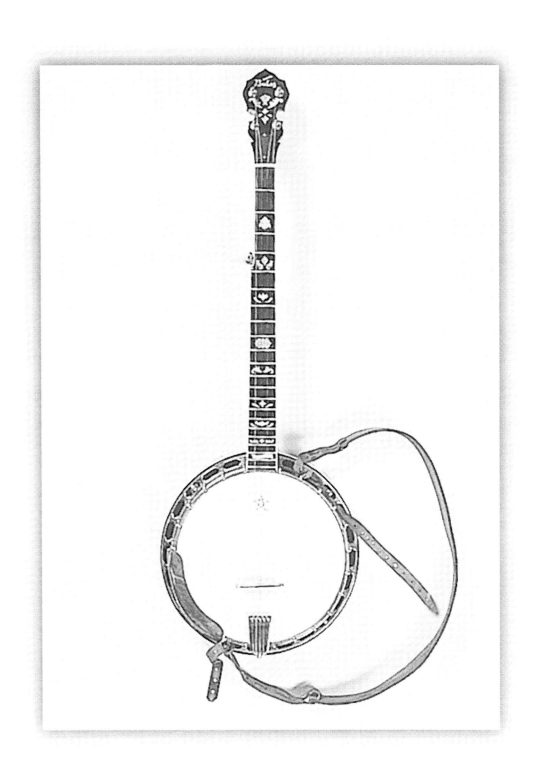

Martin's Waltz

Banjo* (capo 2)

North American

Part A

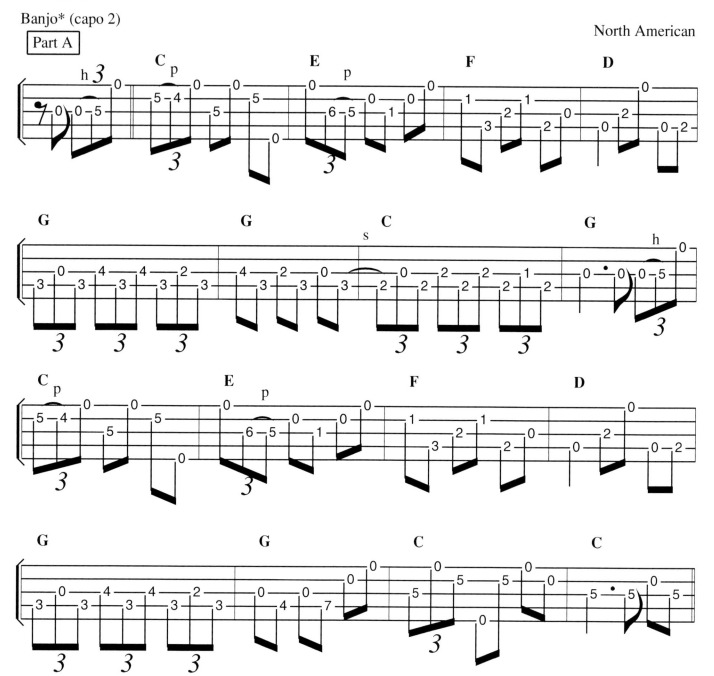

*Banjo is not on CD.

72

Martin's Waltz

Banjo (cont.)

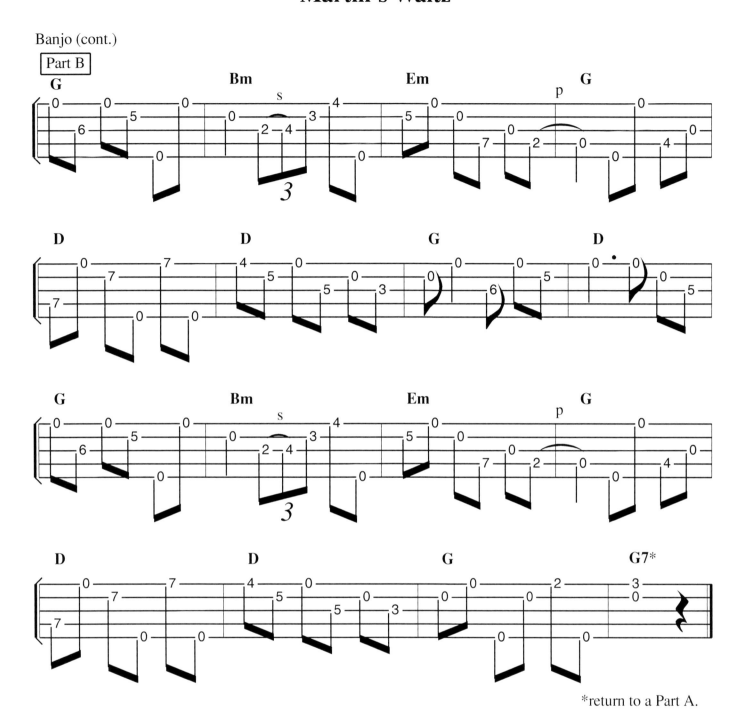

*return to a Part A.

73

Mason's Apron

Banjo* (capo 2)

Irish

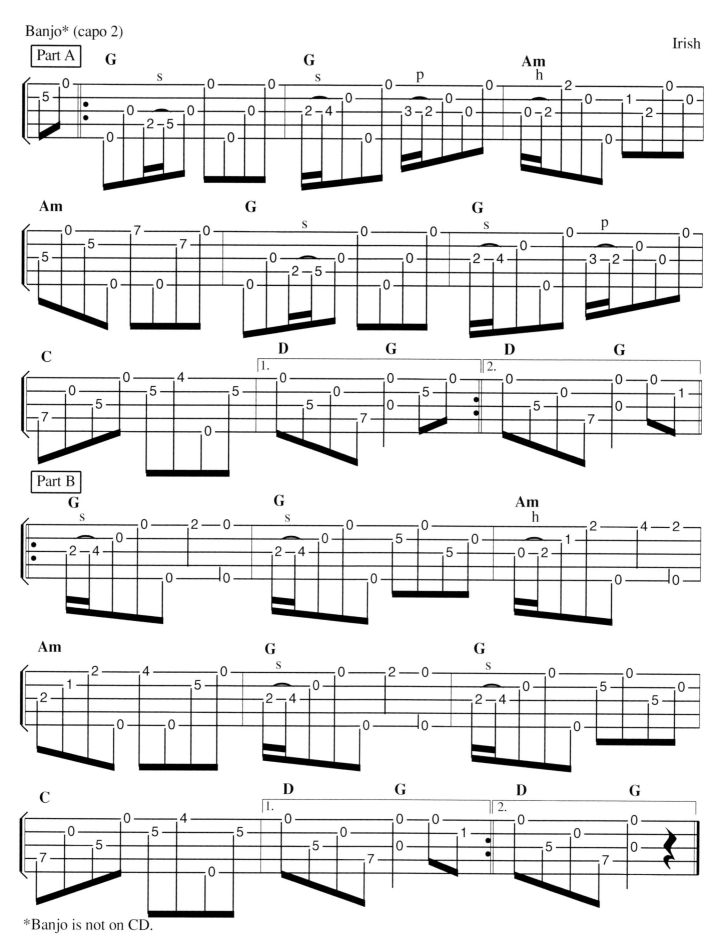

*Banjo is not on CD.

Mississippi Hornpipe

Banjo*

Part A

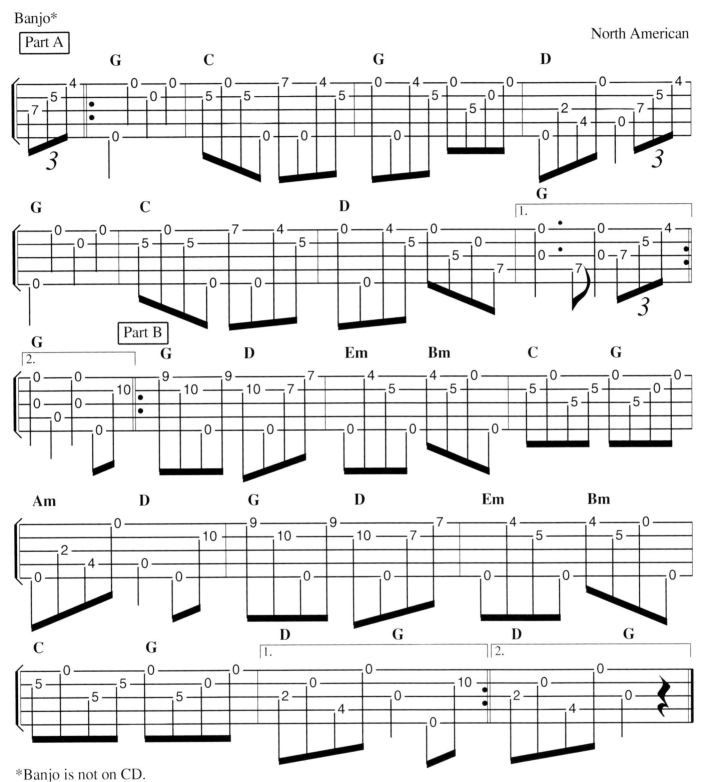

*Banjo is not on CD.

Mississippi Sawyer

Banjo 1*

Part A

North American

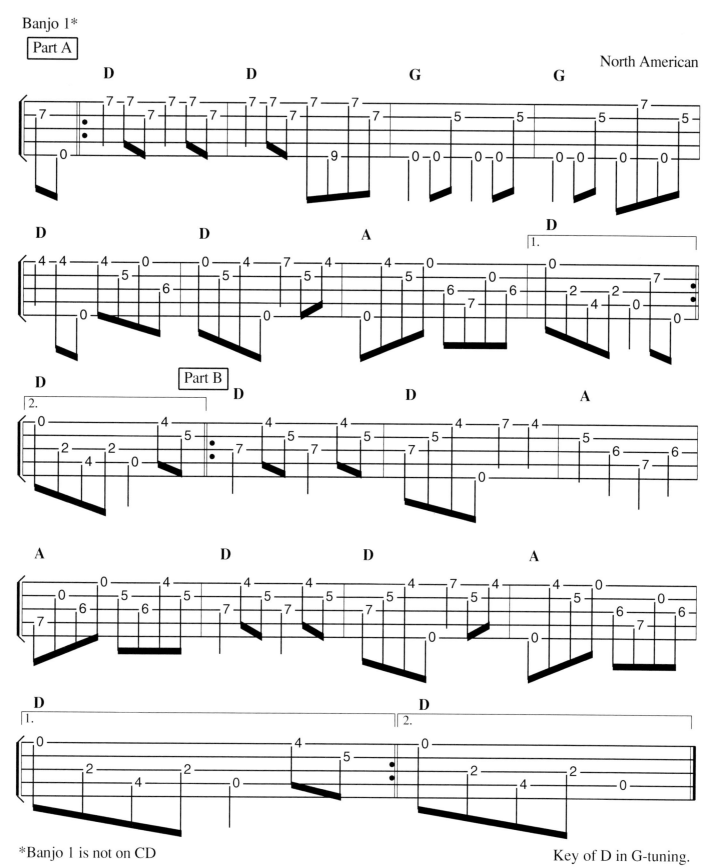

*Banjo 1 is not on CD

Key of D in G-tuning.

Mississippi Sawyer

Banjo 2* (capo 2)

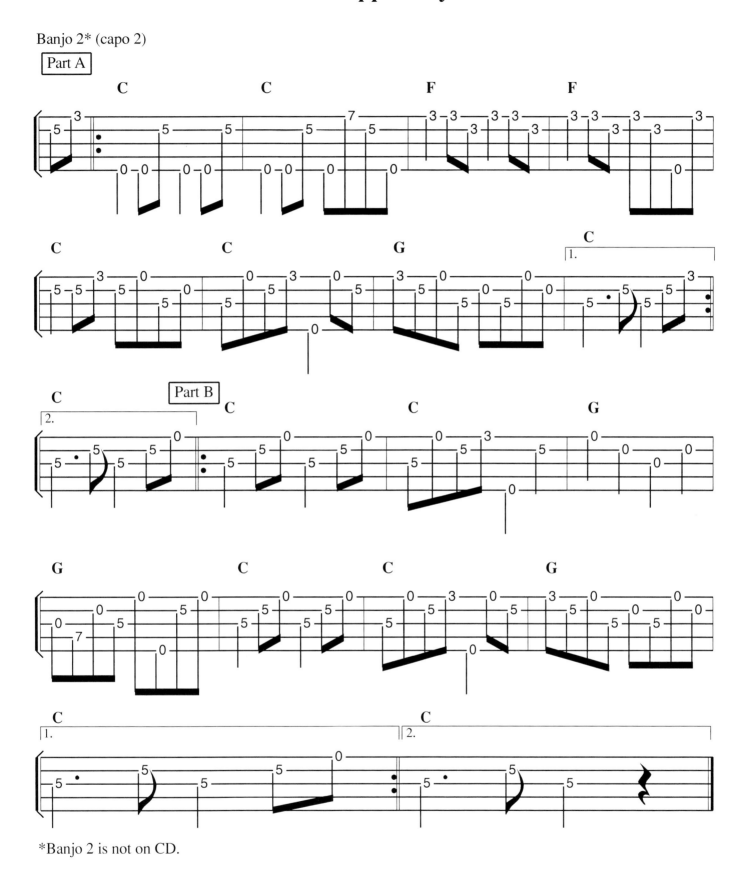

*Banjo 2 is not on CD.

Old Dan Tucker

Banjo* (capo 5)

North American

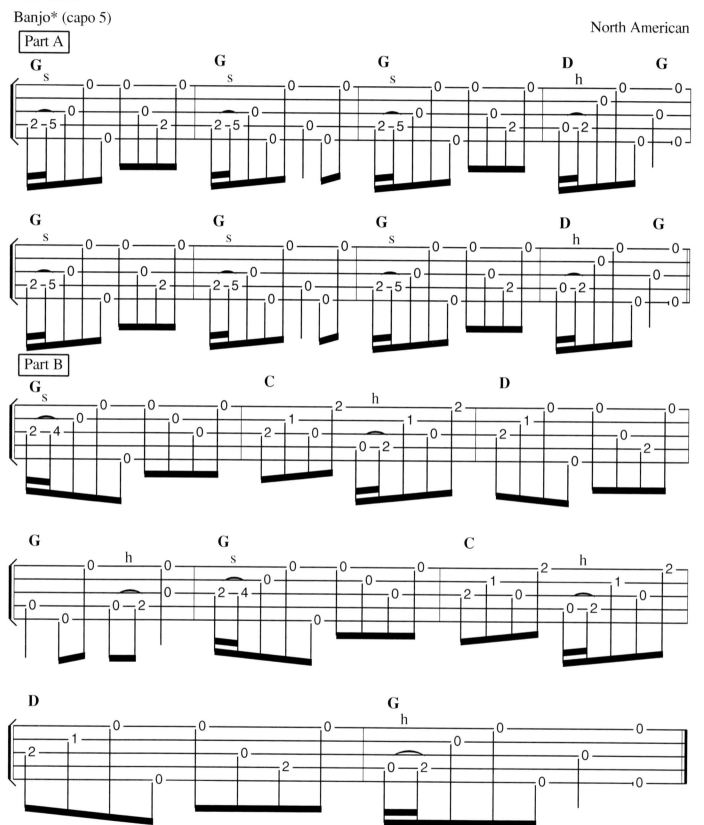

*This banjo part is not on CD.

Old Joe Clark

Banjo (capo 2)

North American

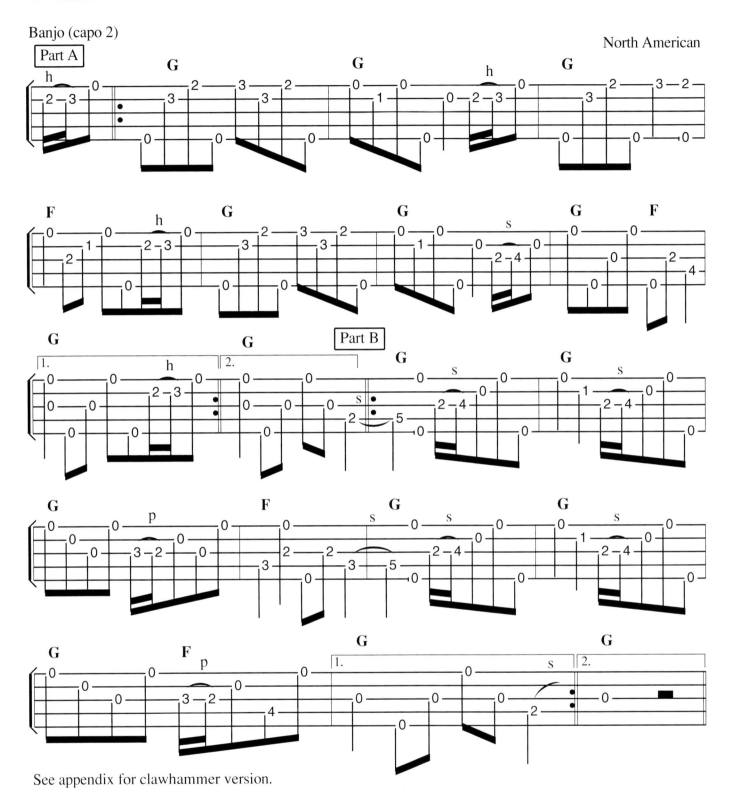

See appendix for clawhammer version.

President Garfield's Hornpipe

Banjo 1* (capo 3)

North American

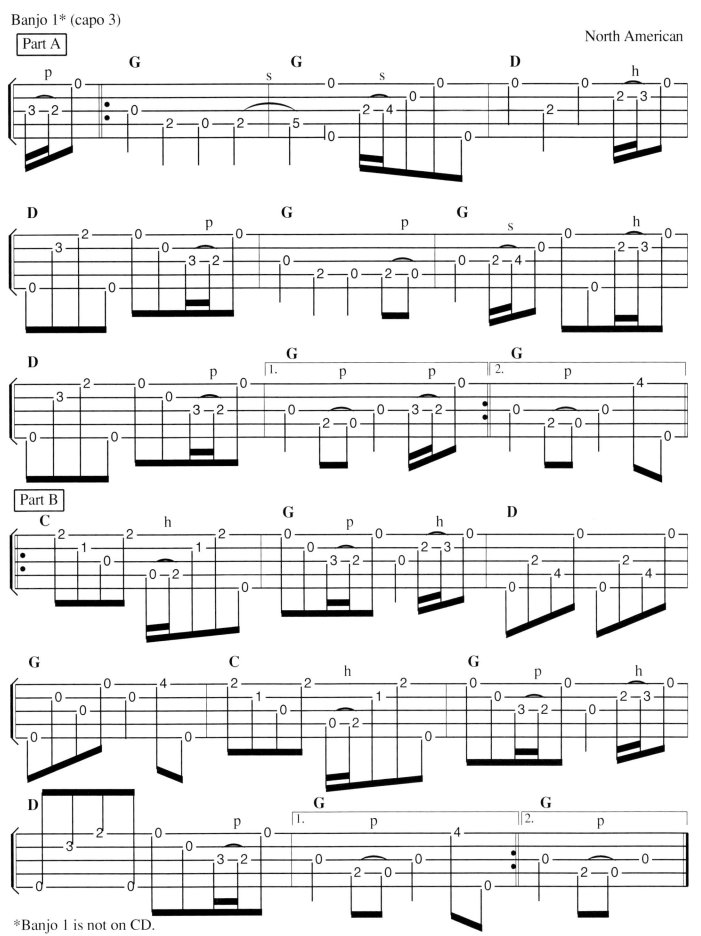

*Banjo 1 is not on CD.

President Garfield's Hornpipe

Banjo 2* (capo 3)

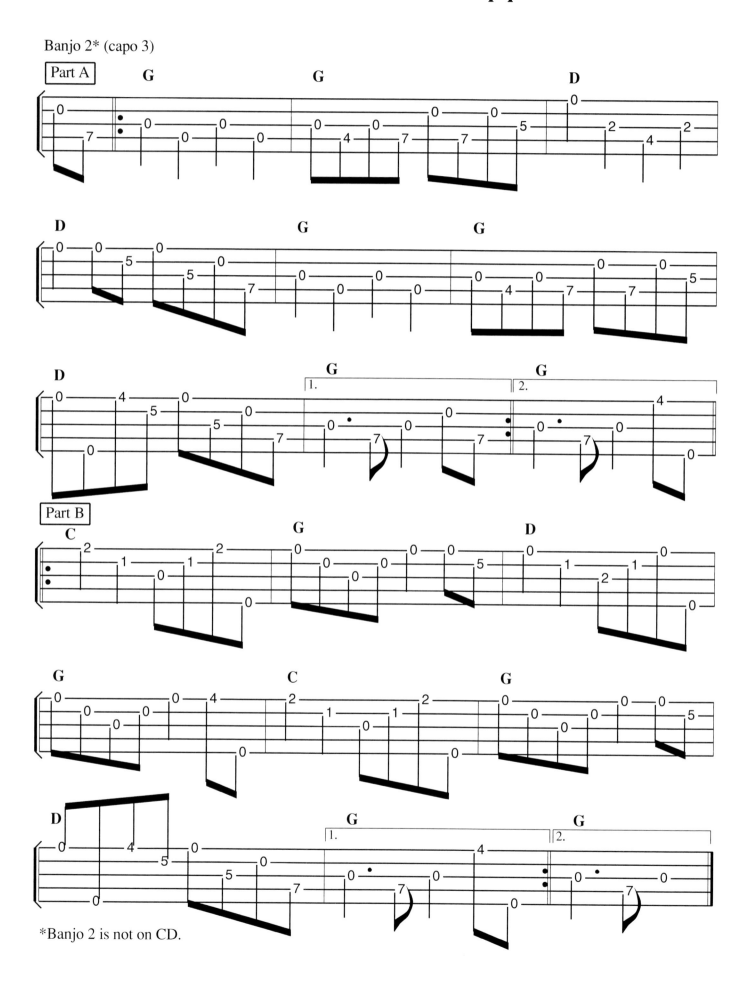

President Garfield's Hornpipe

Banjo 3 (see tuning below)

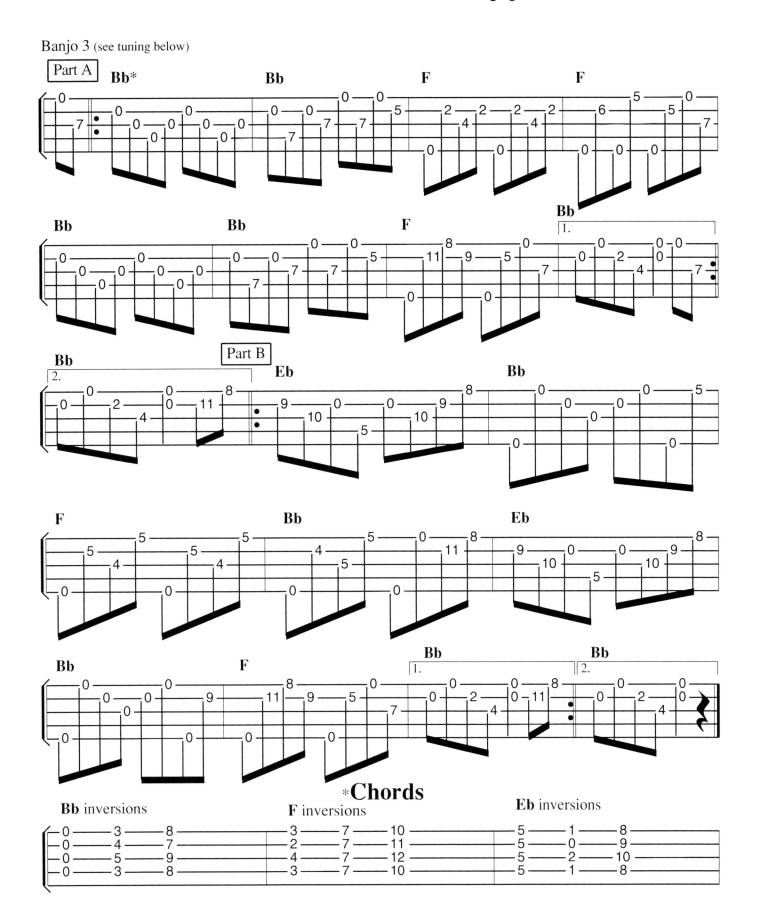

Tune banjo: f, D, F, B♭, D (instead of g, D, G, B, D).

Pretty Peg

Banjo*

Scottish

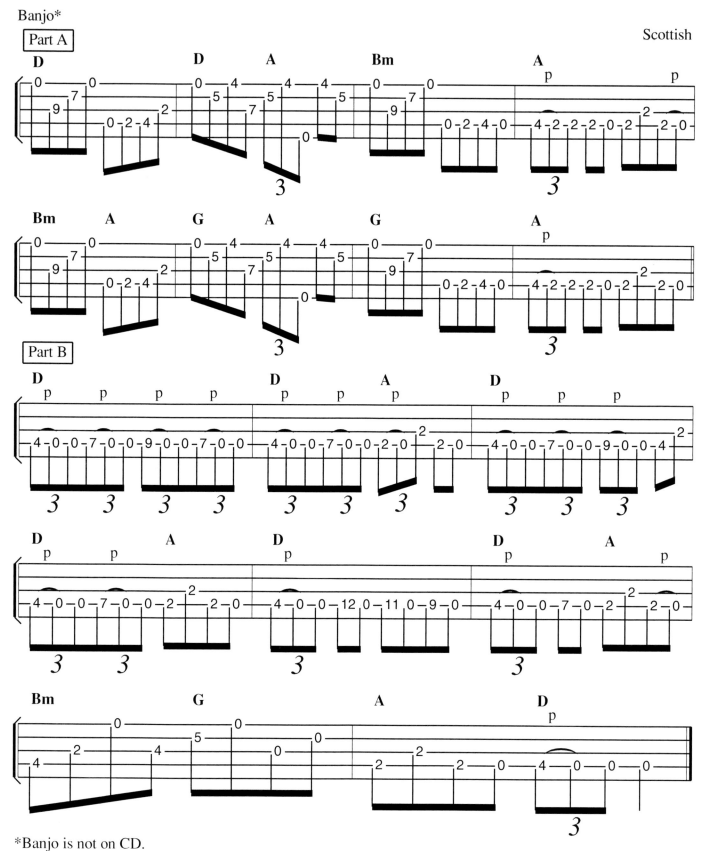

*Banjo is not on CD.

Red-haired Boy

Banjo 1 (capo 2)

Irish

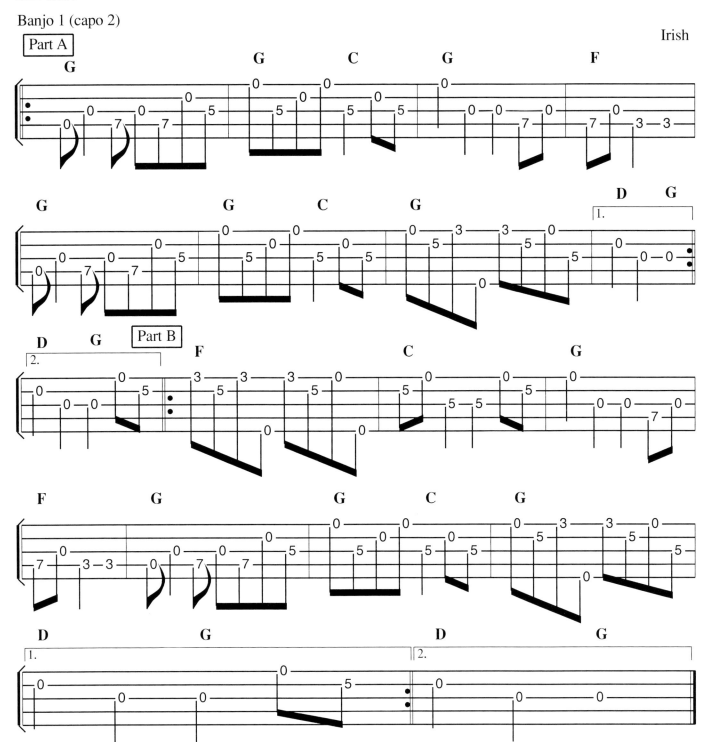

Red-haired Boy

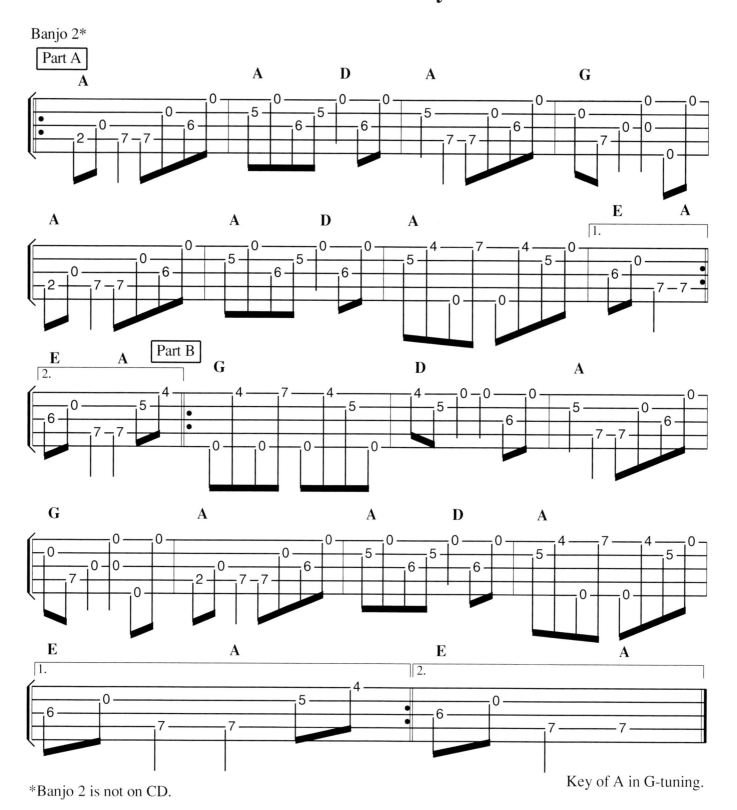

*Banjo 2 is not on CD.

Key of A in G-tuning.

Red-haired Boy

Banjo 3* (capo 2)

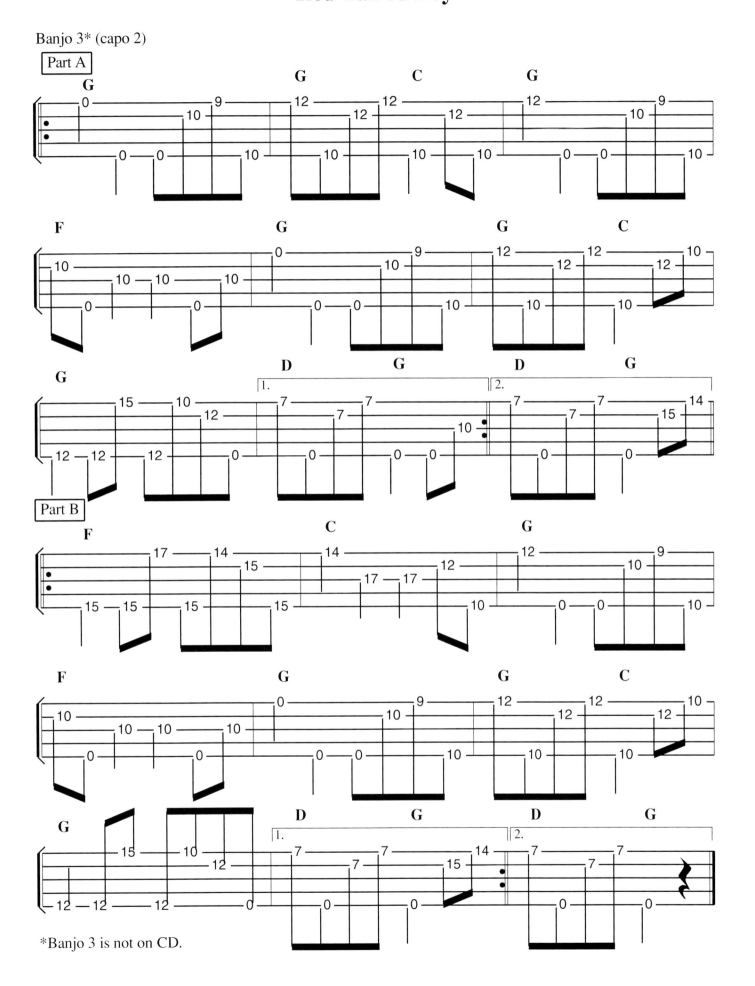

*Banjo 3 is not on CD.

Red Wing

Banjo 1

North American

Part A

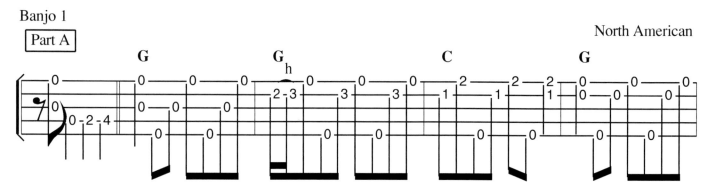
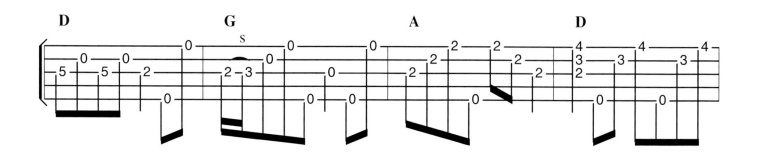
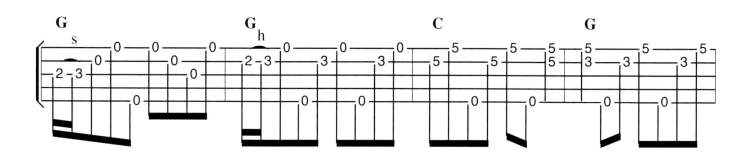
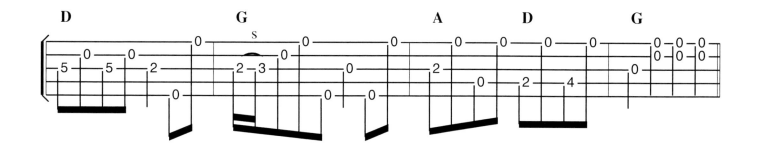

Red Wing

Banjo 1 (cont.)

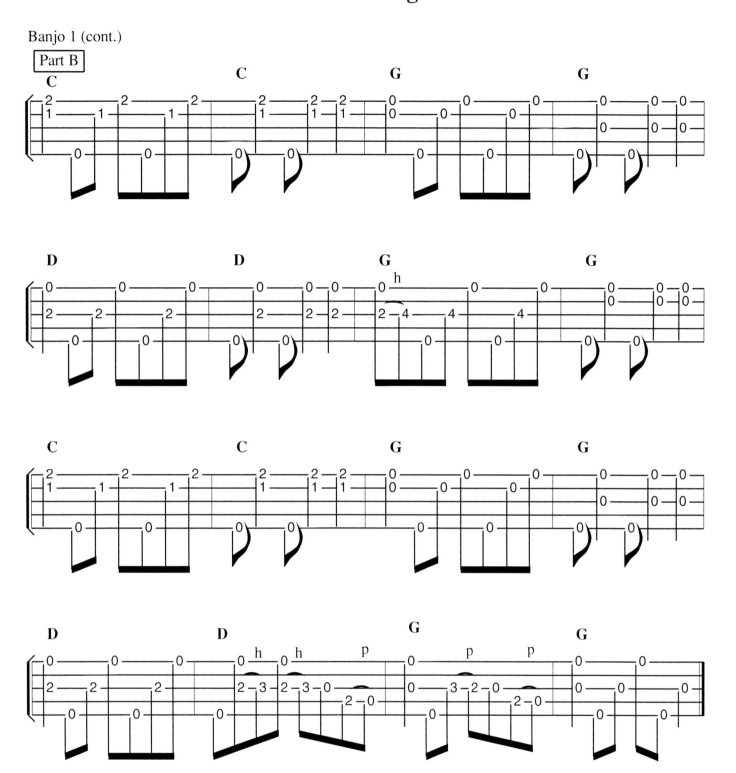

Red Wing

Banjo 2*

Part A

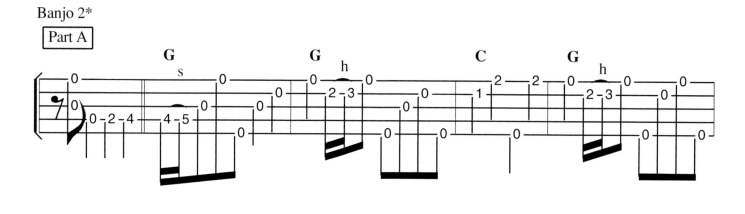

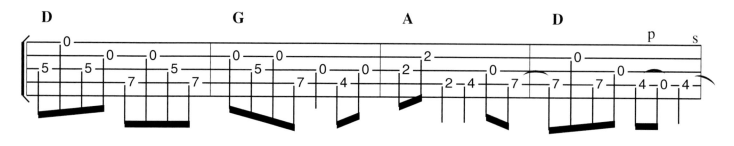

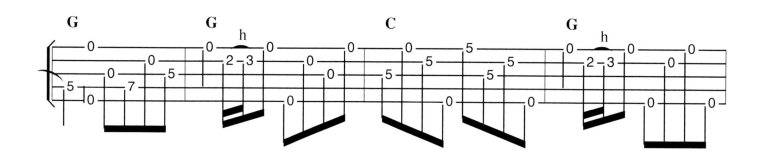

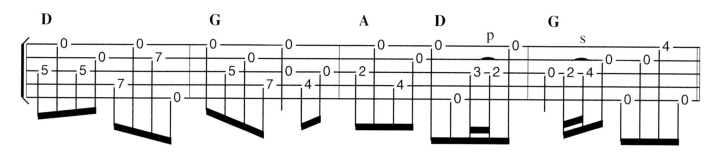

*Banjo 2 is not on CD.

Red Wing

Banjo 2 (cont.)

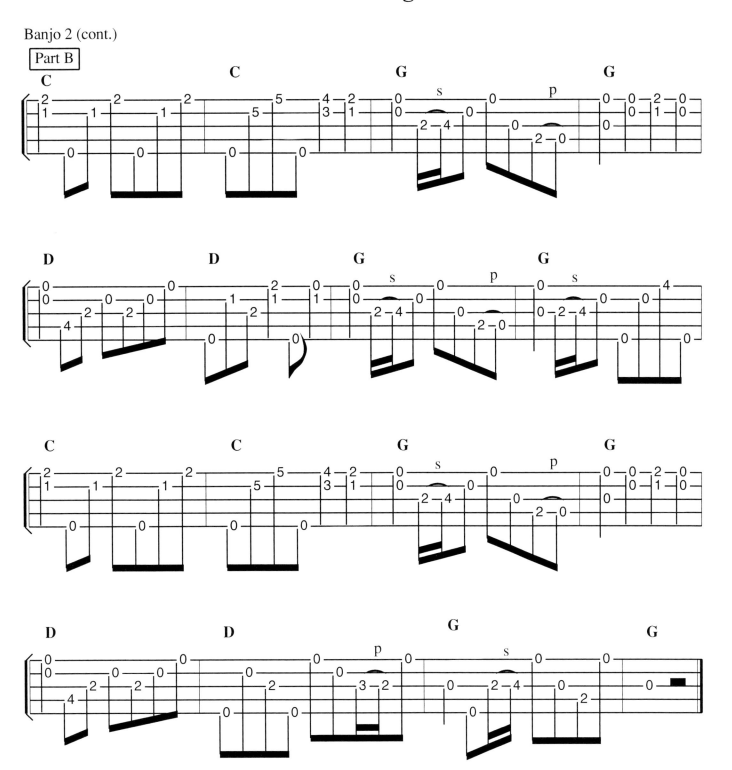

Sailor's Hornpipe

Banjo (capo 3*)

English

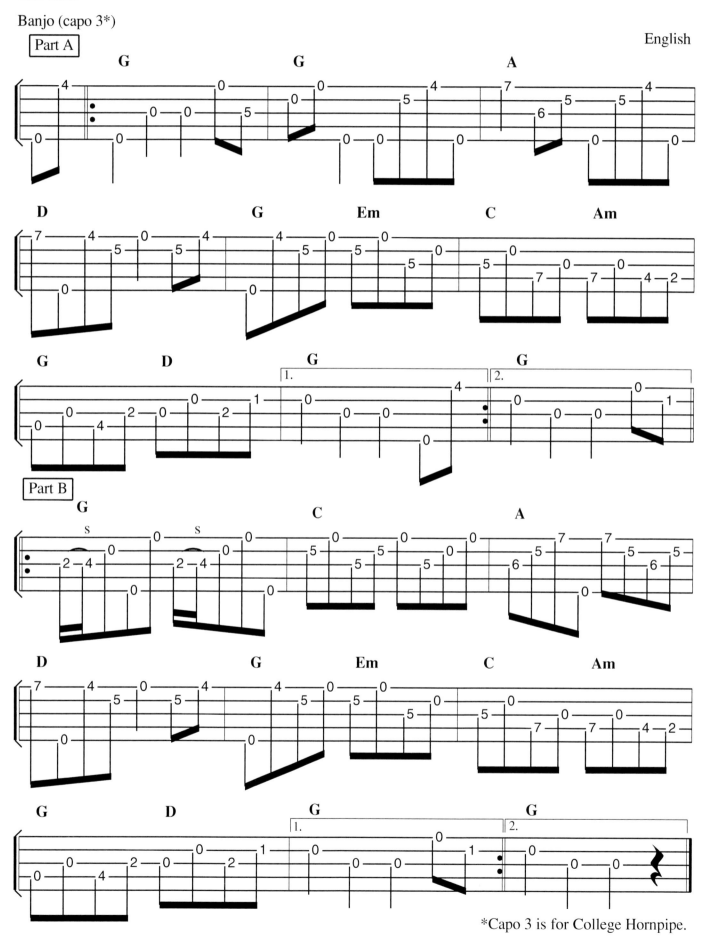

*Capo 3 is for College Hornpipe.

College Hornpipe

Banjo* (capo 3)

North American

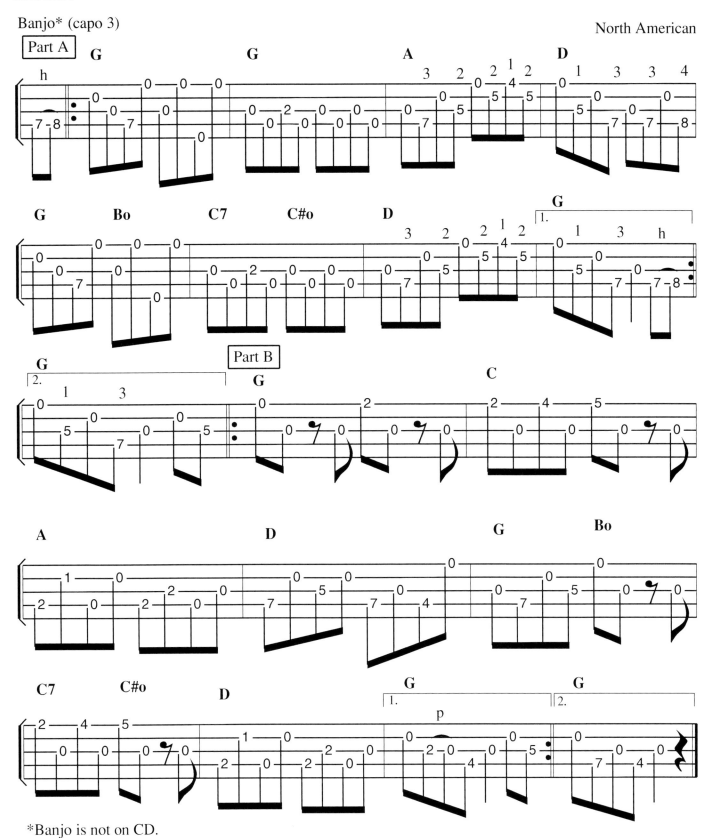

*Banjo is not on CD.

Saint Anne's Reel

Banjo 1*

Irish

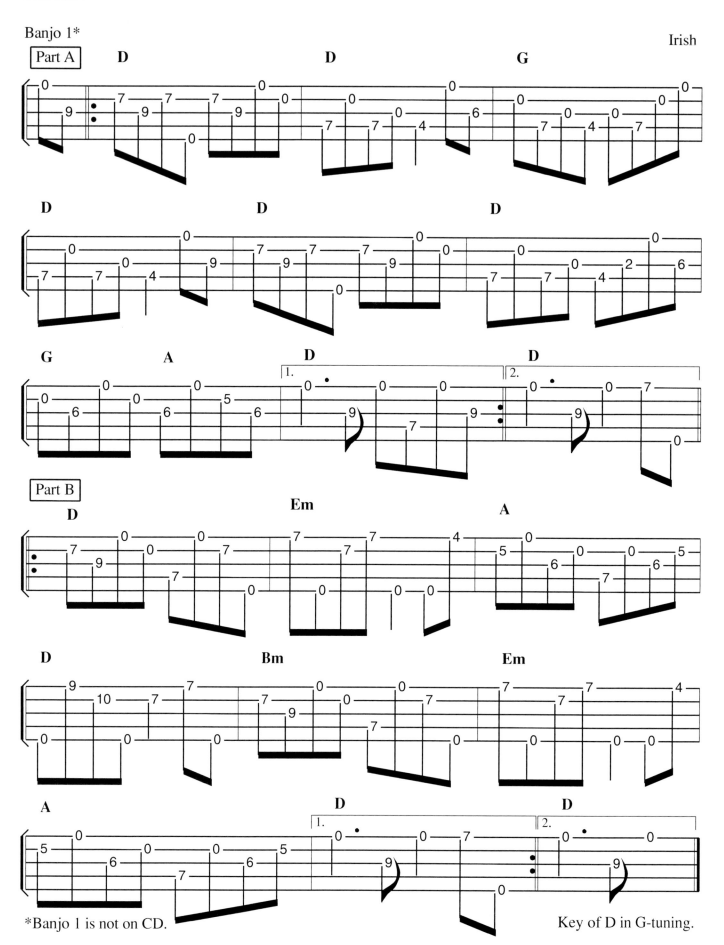

*Banjo 1 is not on CD.

Key of D in G-tuning.

Saint Anne's Reel

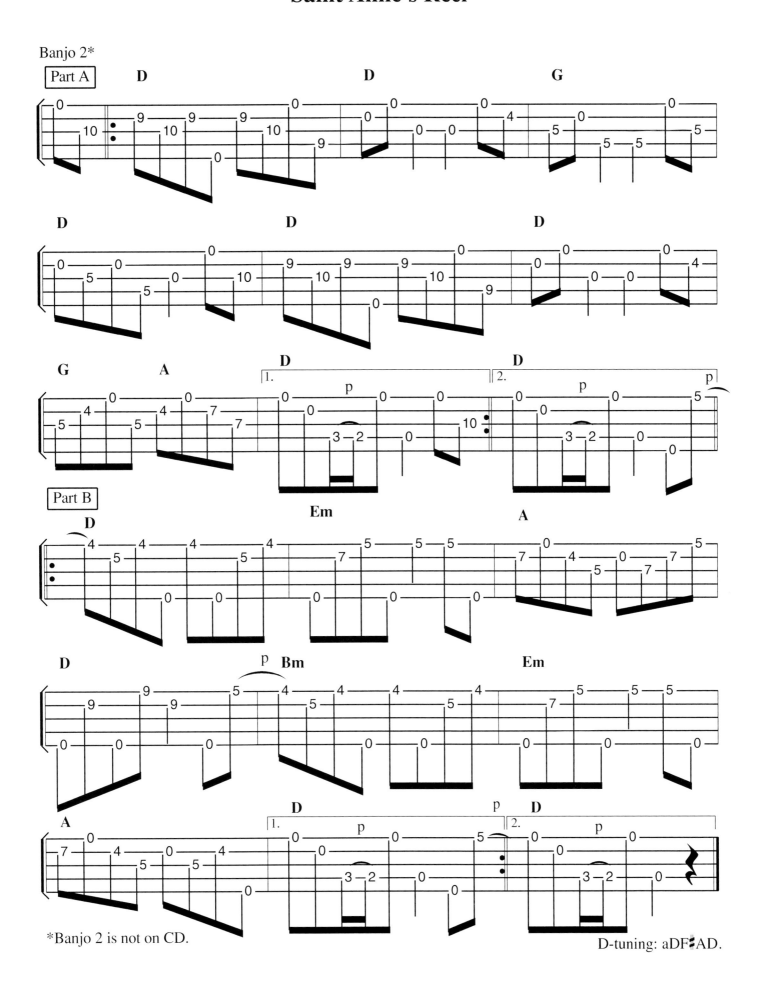

*Banjo 2 is not on CD.

D-tuning: aDF#AD.

Sally Ann

Banjo (capo 2)

North American

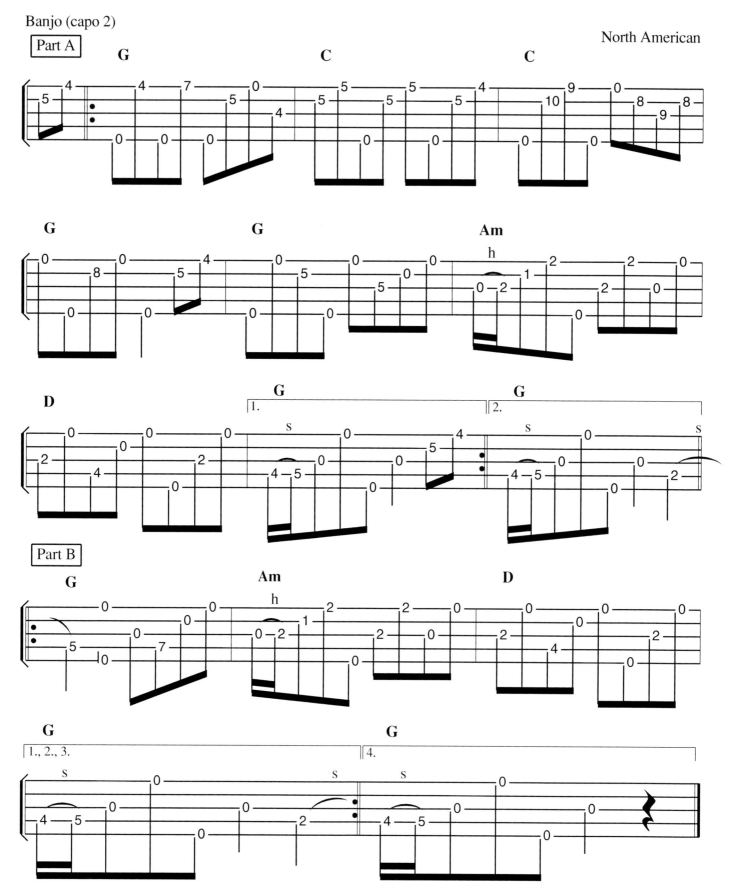

*This page has been
left blank to avoid
awkward page turns.*

Sally Goodin'

Banjo 1 (capo 2)

North American

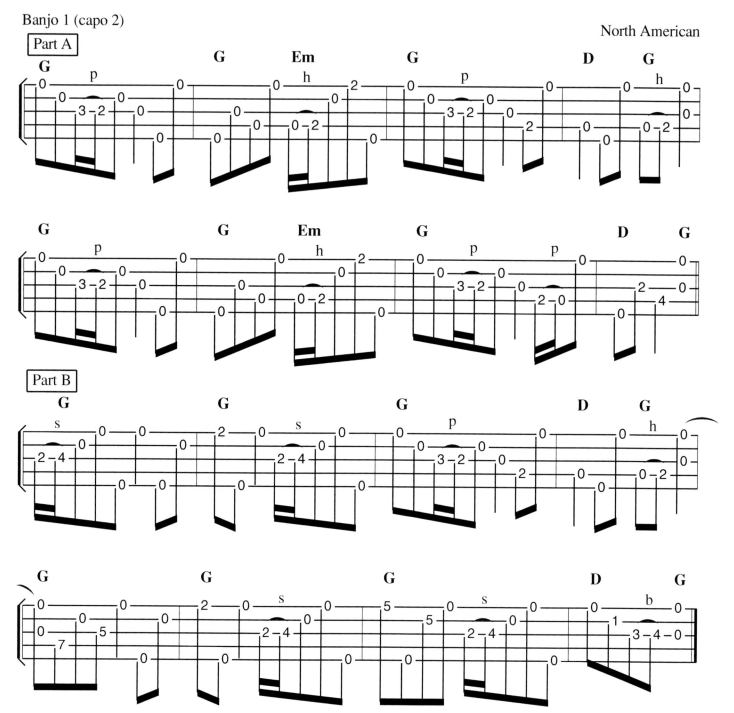

98

Sally Goodin'

Banjo 2* (capo 2)

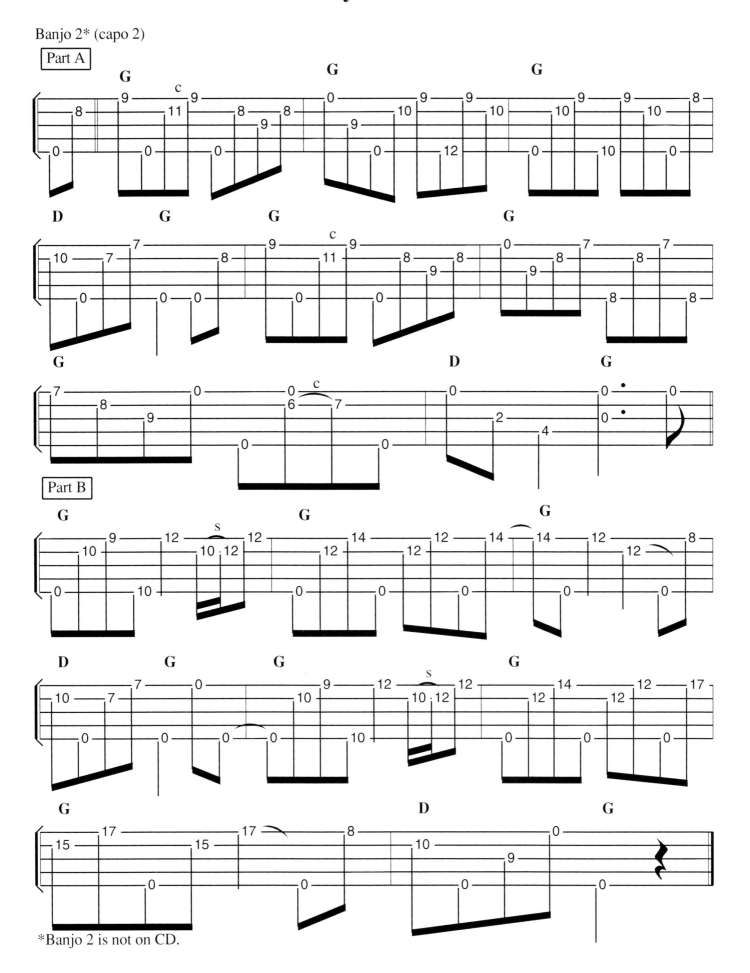

*Banjo 2 is not on CD.

Sally Johnson

Disc 3
Track 7

Banjo 1

North American

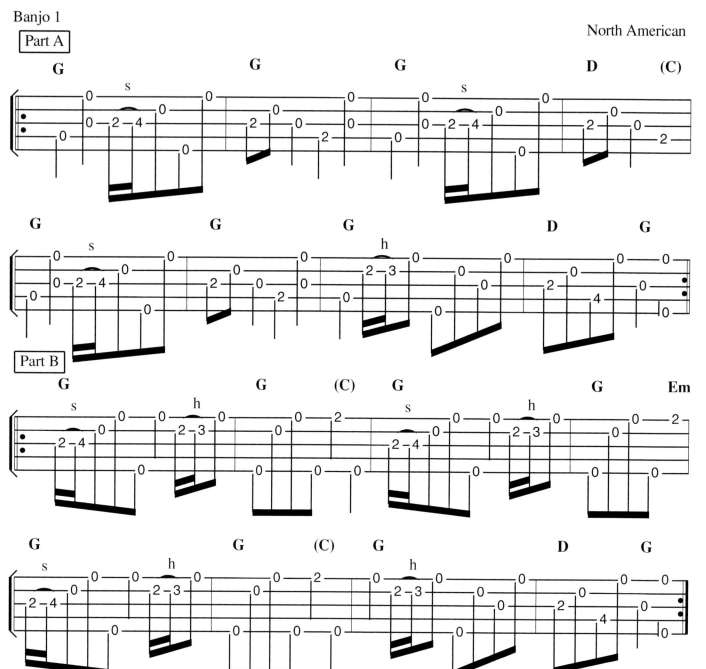

Sally Johnson

Banjo 2*

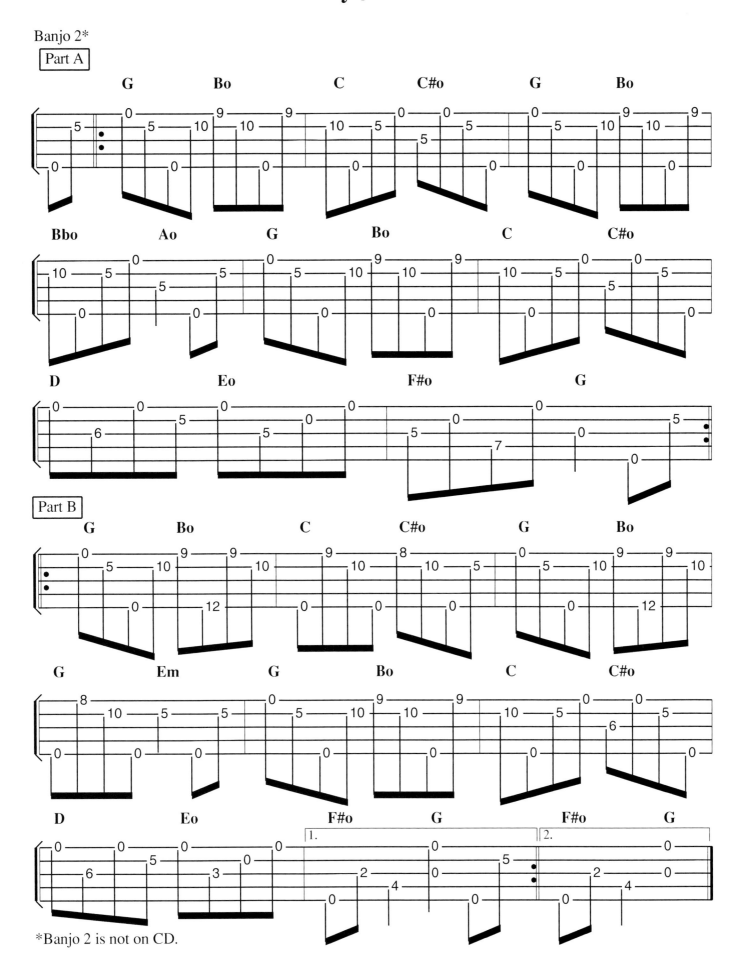

*Banjo 2 is not on CD.

Salt Creek

Banjo 1 (capo 2)

North American

Part A

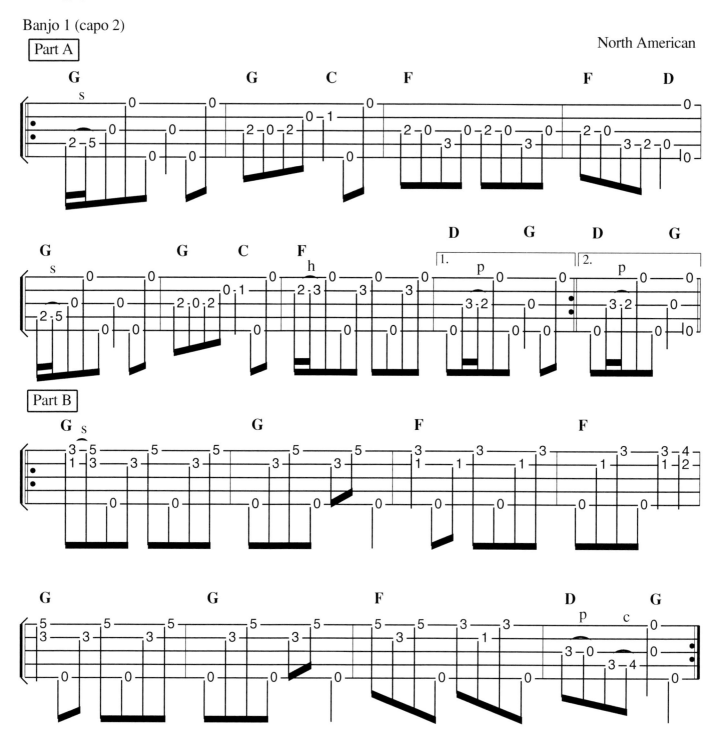

Part B

Salt Creek

Banjo 2* (capo 2)

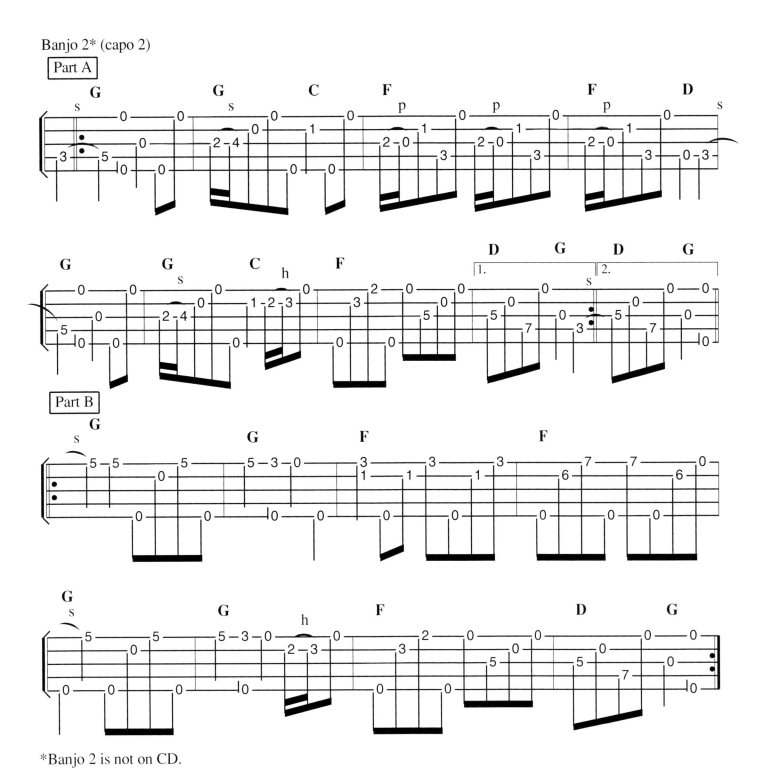

*Banjo 2 is not on CD.

Soldier's Joy

Banjo 1

North American

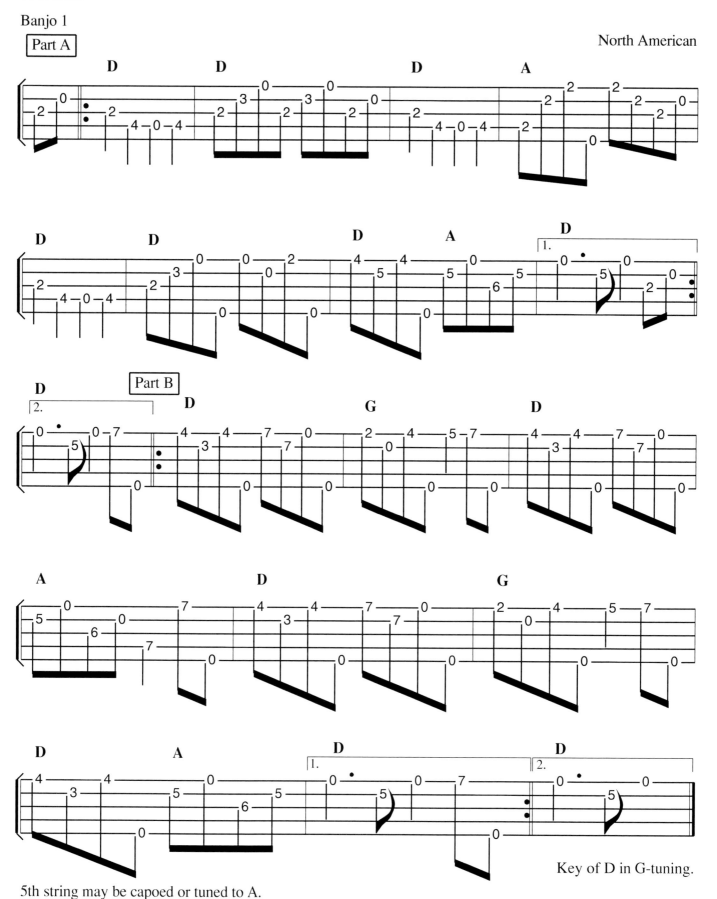

5th string may be capoed or tuned to A.

Key of D in G-tuning.

Soldier's Joy

Banjo 2*

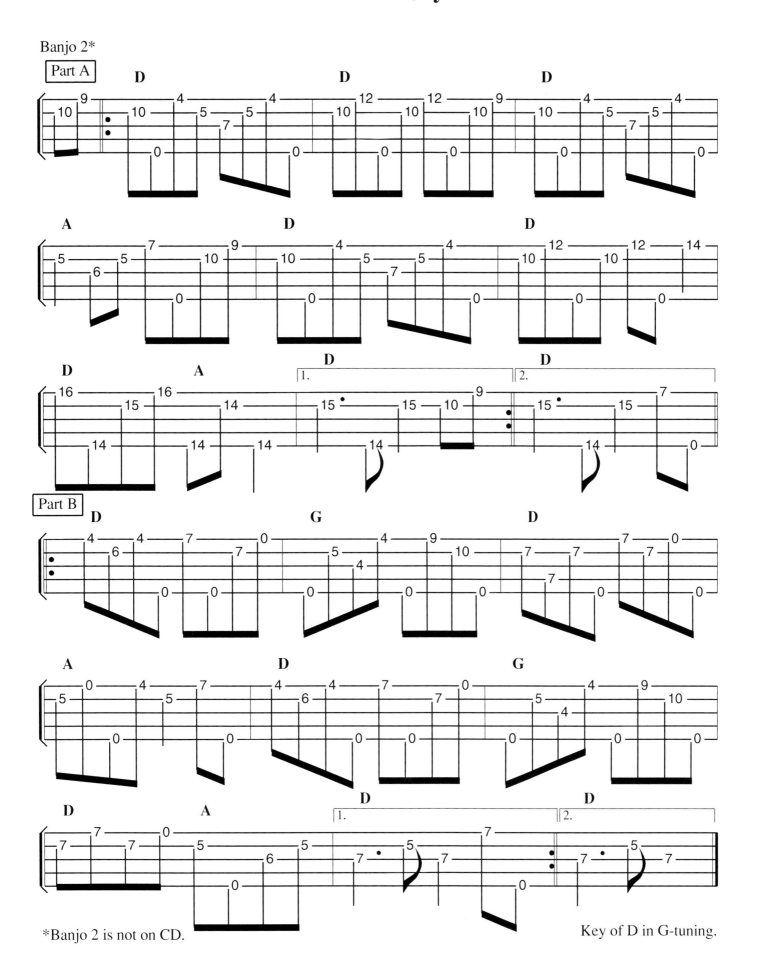

*Banjo 2 is not on CD.

Key of D in G-tuning.

Swallowtail Jig

Banjo*

Irish

Part A

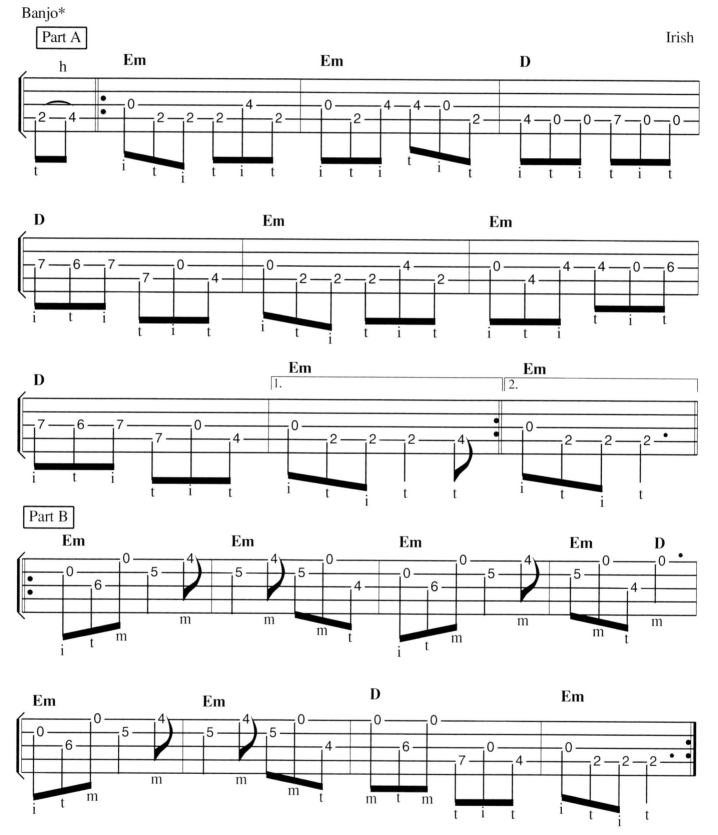

Part B

*Banjo is not on CD.

Temperance Reel

Banjo 1

North American

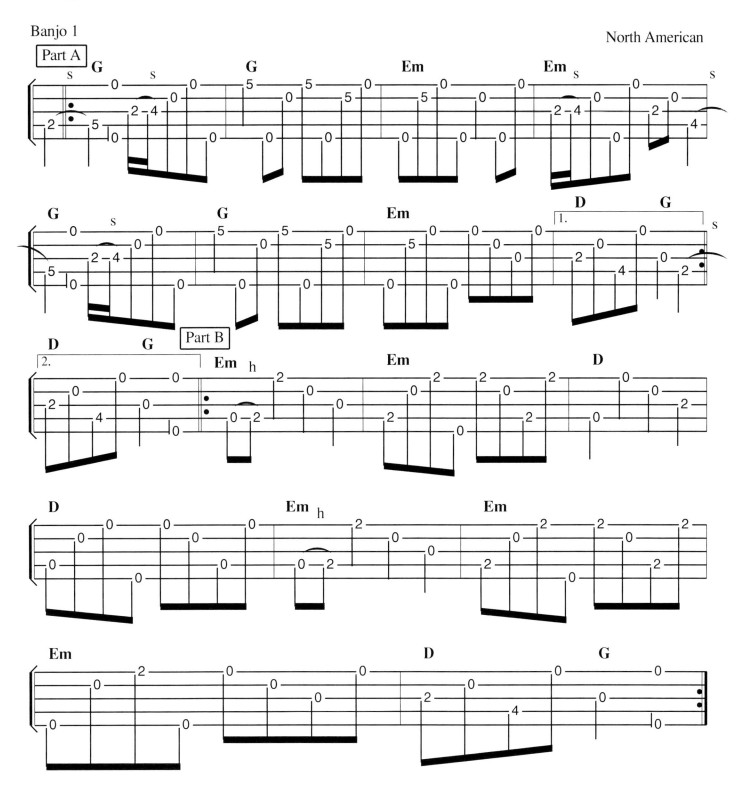

Temperance Reel

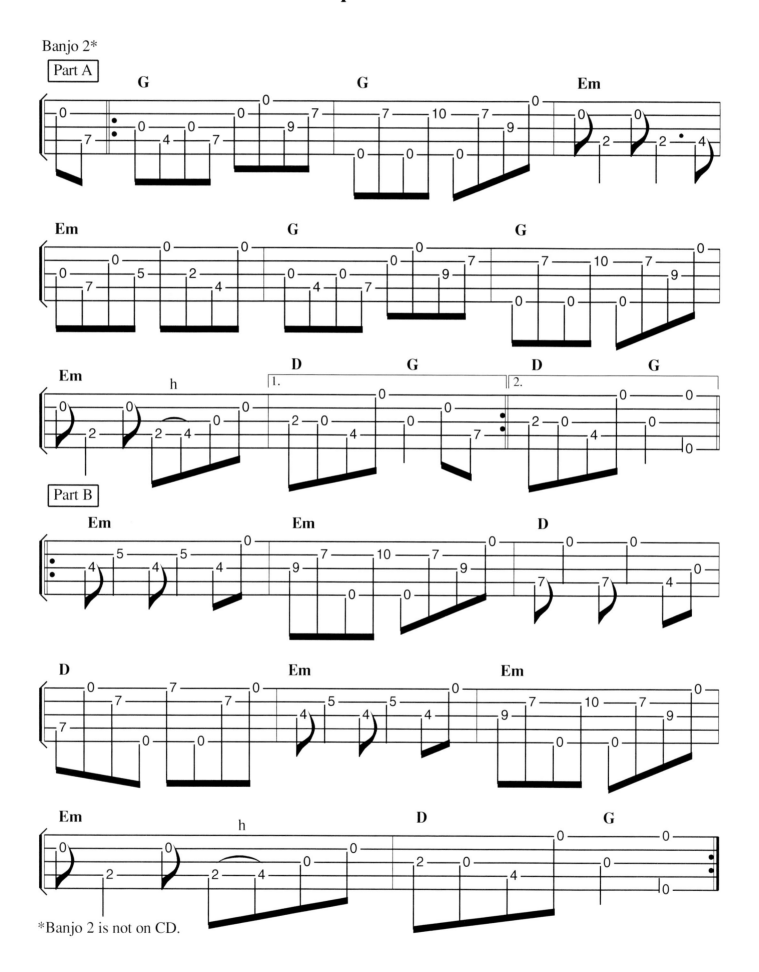

Banjo 2*

Part A

Part B

*Banjo 2 is not on CD.

Temperance Reel

Banjo 3*

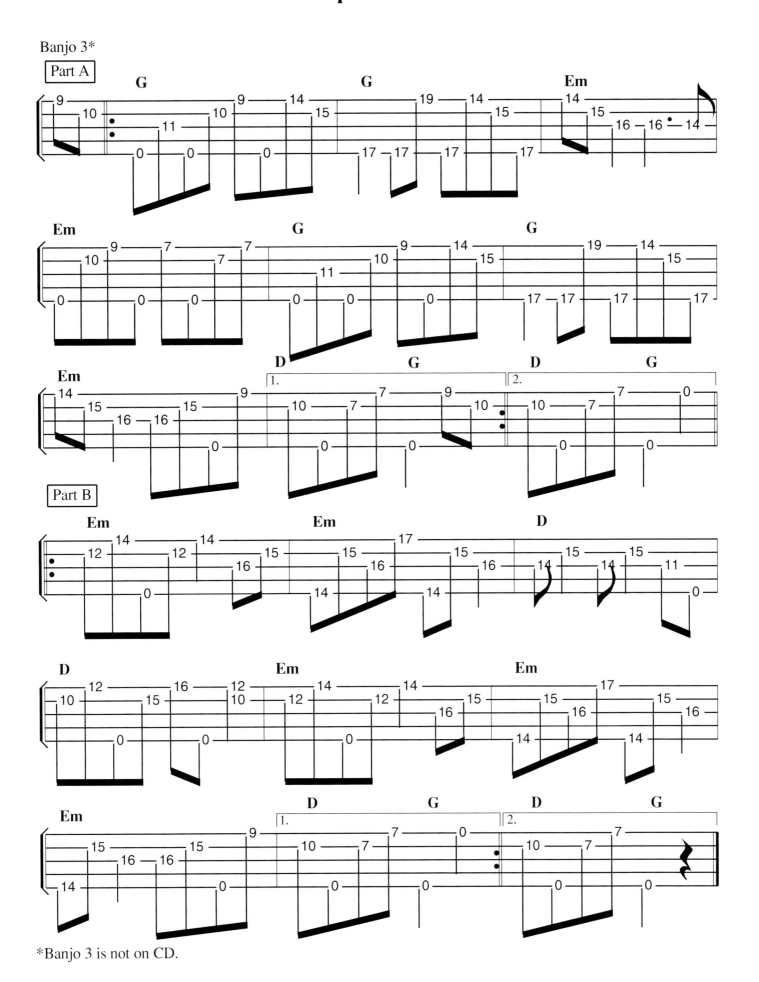

*Banjo 3 is not on CD.

Tom and Jerry

Banjo 1 (capo 2)

North American

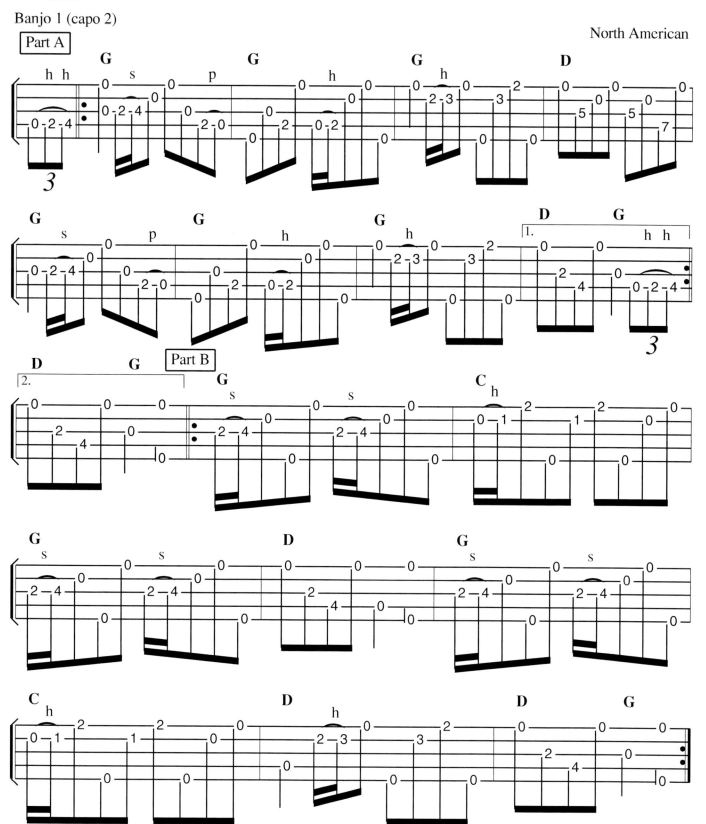

Tom and Jerry

Banjo 2* (capo 2)

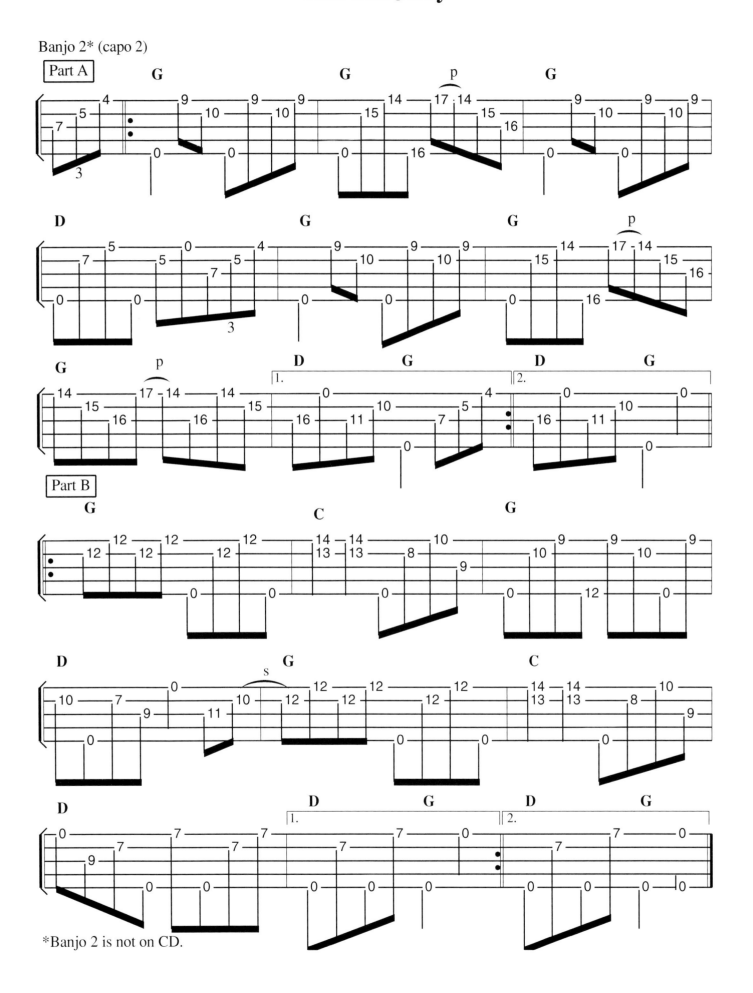

*Banjo 2 is not on CD.

Turkey in the Straw

Banjo 1

North American

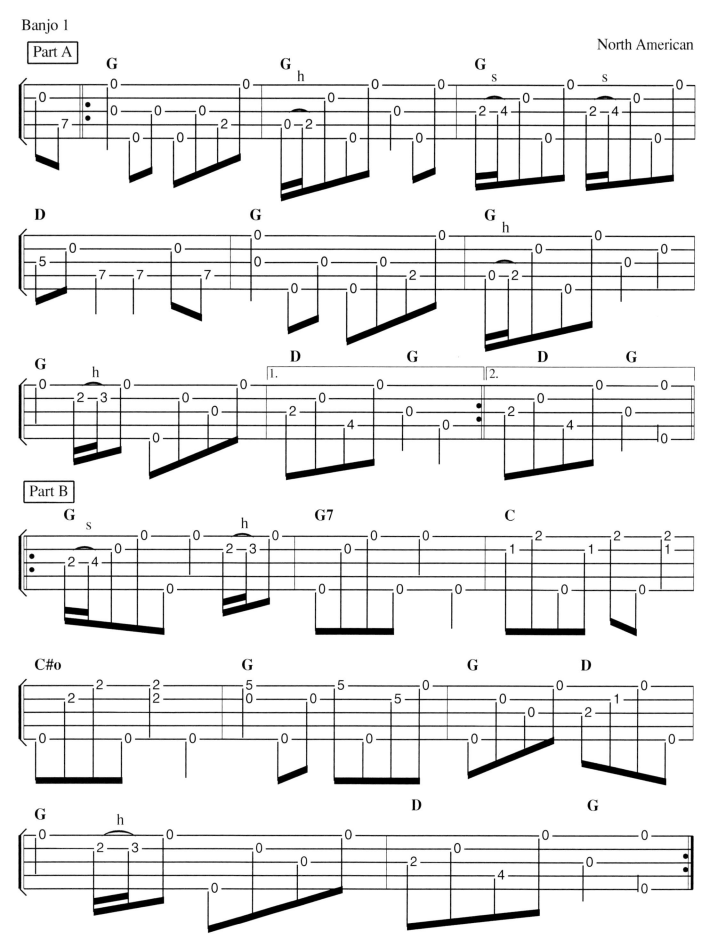

Turkey in the Straw

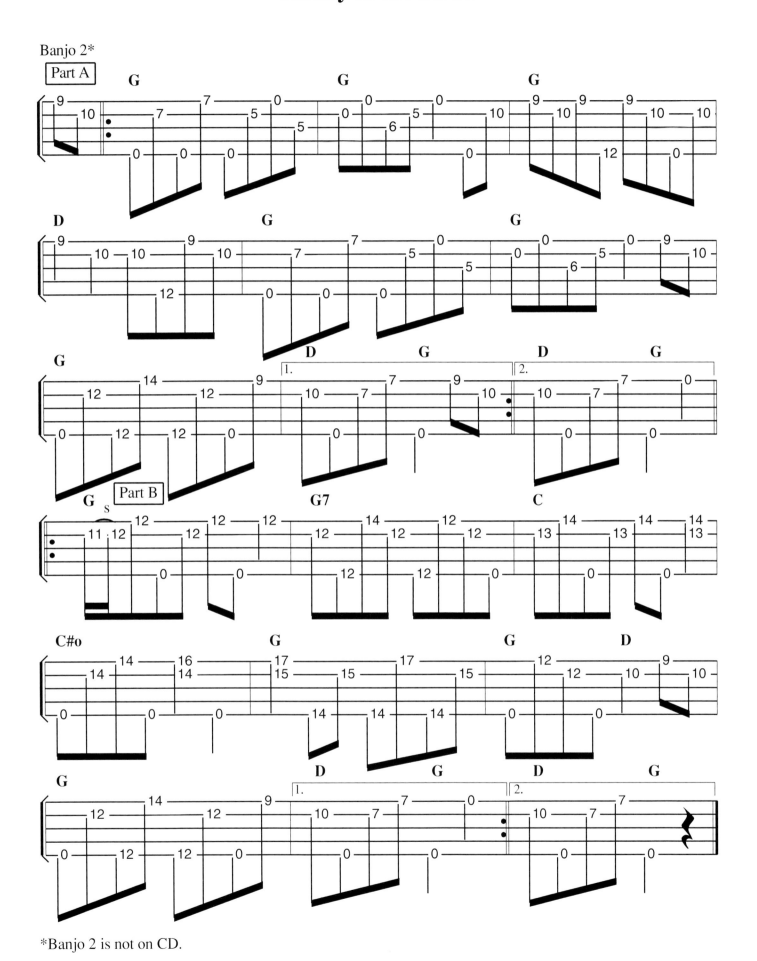

*Banjo 2 is not on CD.

Uncle Joe

Banjo (capo 2)*

Scotland

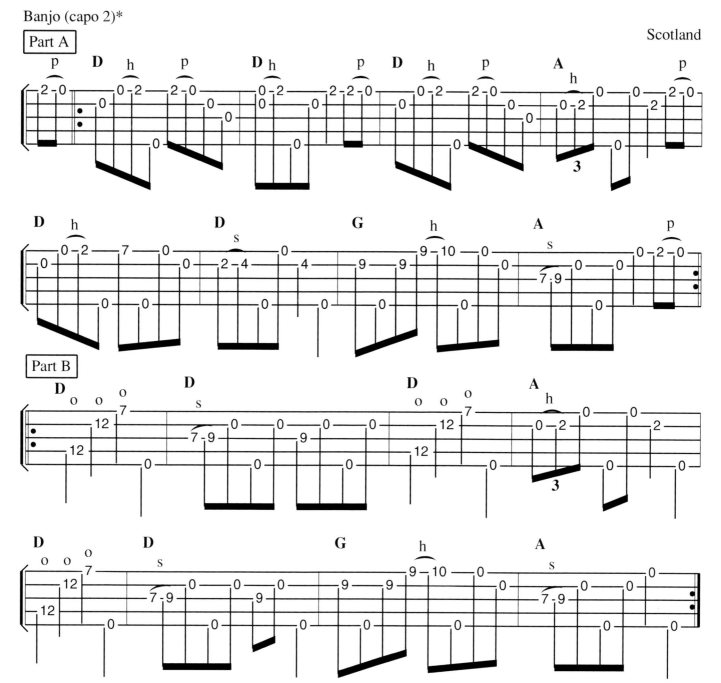

*Tune banjo: gCGCD (capo 2 for high g-string also).

Under the Double Eagle

Banjo*

Part A

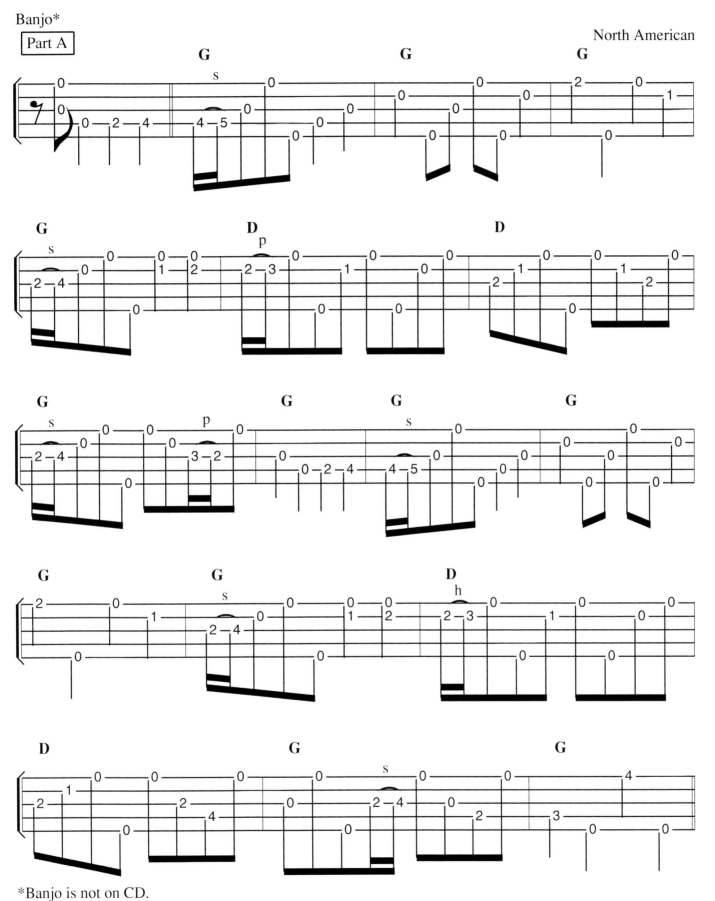

*Banjo is not on CD.

Under the Double Eagle

Banjo (cont.)

Part B

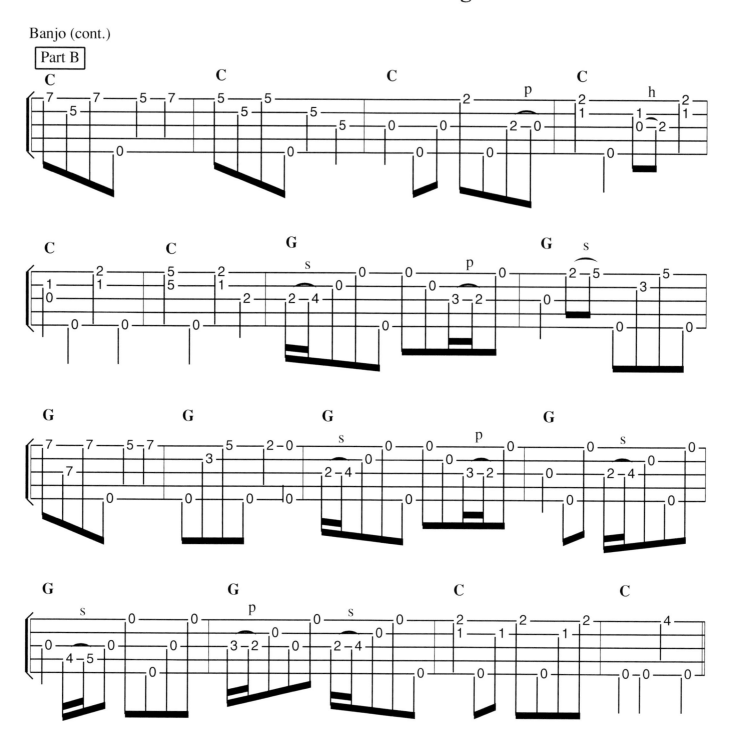

Under the Double Eagle

Banjo (part B cont.)

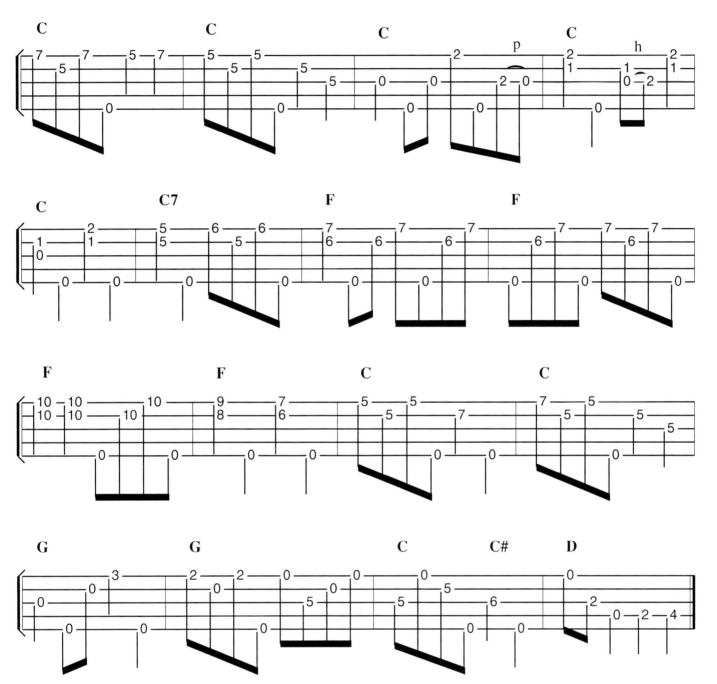

117

Whiskey Before Breakfast

Banjo 1*

Scottish

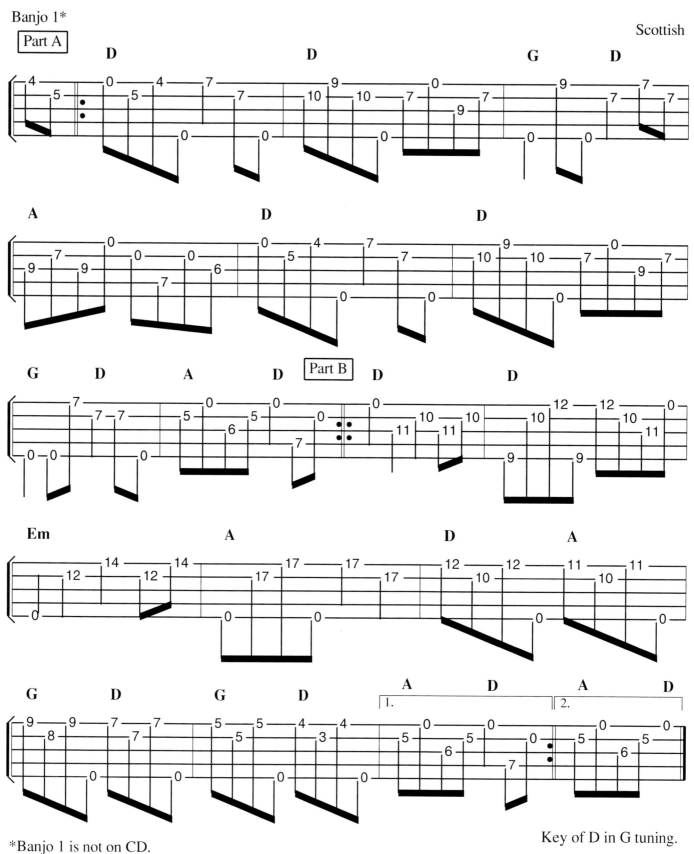

*Banjo 1 is not on CD.

Key of D in G tuning.

118

Whiskey Before Breakfast

Banjo 2*

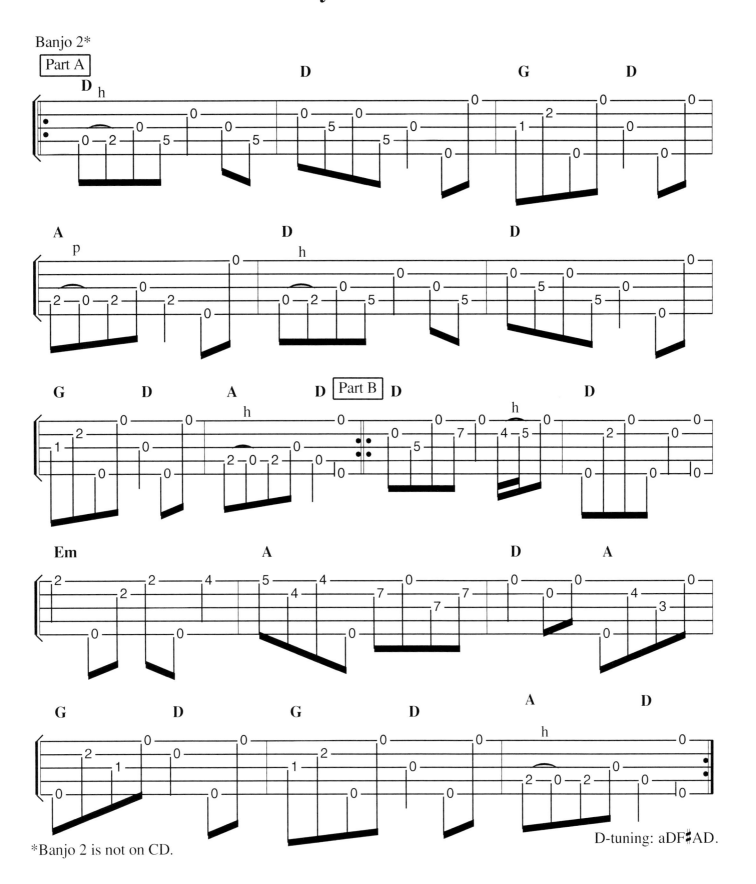

*Banjo 2 is not on CD.

D-tuning: aDF#AD.

119

This page has been
left blank to avoid
awkward page turns.

Appendix

Picking

The 5-string banjo is a right hand intensive instrument. The right hand uses many roll patterns and variations that must become second nature for the player to become fluent on the instrument. Because of the need to train the right hand, the next few pages will deal with these rolls. Each roll pattern should be studied and practiced until it becomes smooth and strong before speeding it up. In this book the right (or picking) hand fingers will be indicated by the following symbols:

t	=	Thumb
i	=	Index
m	=	Middle

The thumb typically plucks the 5th, 4th, 3rd and occasionally the 2nd strings. The index finger plucks the 2nd, 3rd and occasionally the 4th strings. The middle finger plucks the 1st and on occasion, the 2nd strings. The playing of 2 consecutive 8th notes with the same picking finger will seldom occur in this book and typically happens only in slow tunes.

BE SURE to practice rolls, and eventually the tunes, with precision. The general rule is this: *If you practice mistakes, you will become very good at mistakes! If you practice correctly, you will play correctly!*

The picks

It is important that you place your picking hand on the banjo head in a comfortable position. The ends of the picks should be twisted or rotated until they strike the strings squarely. Rather than contorting the hand, which may impede progress and speed, it is usually better to contort (or adjust) the picks and keep the hand relaxed.

IMPORTANT NOTE: Except for a few tricky sections, the tunes in this book will not show the right (or picking) hand fingering (t, i, m). Therefore, careful study of the rolls and guidelines in this appendix is suggested.

The following pages of this appendix should help you understand how to read tablature and also show you exercises that are intended to prepare the picking hand for the tunes in this book. Be Sure to work these exercises thoroughly before beginning with the tunes in the book.

Left hand banjo tablature symbols:

s = **Slide** - Sliding a finger from a note to a higher note; or sliding from a note to a lower note. The sliding finger should maintain full pressure on the string throughout the slide motion in order for the notes to be loud.

h = **Hammer-on** - Like when a hammer hits a nail, a finger hits a note and makes it ring without being plucked by the pick. The note that is hammered should be as loud as any plucked note.

p = **Pull-off** - This is more like flipping the string with a finger on the fingering hand (as opposed to the picking hand). The note that is pulled-off (or flipped) should be as loud as any plucked note.

b	=	**Bend** - This is done by bending the string at a particular note (push the string upward and then bring it back into place). If possible, use the ring finger, assisted by the middle and index fingers, to better control the bend. This practice places less strain on the ring finger—especially on acoustic guitars.
c	=	**Choke** - The same thing as a bend. Banjo players usually say "choke" while guitar players say "bend."

Chords and Rhythm

Chords are a very vital part of banjo playing. When playing with other people the banjo player will play the melody (or solo) quite frequently but, when not playing the solo, the banjo player will likely play chords in a particular rhythm. In Bluegrass music, for example, it is especially important to emphasize the offbeat during mandolin solos, since this is usually the job of the mandolin player. Otherwise the banjo player will quietly play roll patterns with chords, always being conscious not to cover up the vocalist or the soloist. This is especially relevant when the guitarist is soloing. As you advance, you will also learn to add appropriate 'fills' in the spaces between vocal parts and to punctuate the end of phrases.

Moving from chord to chord

The most difficult part of playing chords is getting the fingering hand to move from one chord to the next chord rapidly. Since chords are made up of several notes played at once, it becomes necessary to use more than one finger to play a chord. Making several fingers move quickly from one position to a completely new position requires practice. The exercise that will best help this ability to develop is one that forces the fingers to move quickly from chord to chord. The following exercise steps will prove very helpful:

Step 1: Learn the following 5 chords (A, D, F, C, E).

Step 2: Place the fingers on the first chord "A."

Step 3: With someone's help, or with a clock in front of you, see how many times you can play all 5 chords in the space 1 minute. You can strum each chord once making sure that all strings are ringing clearly.

Step 4: Count your results. If you were able to play all 5 chords 6 times plus 3 chords of a 7th time, you got a score of 6.3. If you were able to play all 5 chords 8 times plus 1 chord of a 9th time, you got a score of 8.1. The goal is to get a 12.0 because at 12.0 you are changing chords once every second!

Chord Diagrams and Inversions

Chord diagrams and charts of some (not all) of the most used and most practical chords for the banjo are shown later in this appendix. Get to know these chords well and you will be much better prepared to play with other people. The chords diagrams in this appendix also show major and minor inversions for the G, D, B♭ and Cm tunings found in this book. Any major or minor chord can be found by moving these shapes up or down the fingerboard to the appropriate location. These chords can be used for accompaniment, arranging or improvisational ideas.

Keys and Tunings

The 5-string banjo is traditionally a 'key of G' instrument. Many banjo players use a capo to change keys rather than actually playing in specific keys like A, F or D. Most of the tunes in this book are arrangements of fiddle tunes. The most the common keys for fiddle tunes are A, D and G with a smaller number of tunes played in C, F and B♭.

Other keys are also used, but to a lesser degree. In order to become more proficient at creating your own arrangements that, like many of the melodies in this book, are made up predominantly of eighth notes, you may find the following information helpful.

Key of G

Open G-tuning (**gDGBD**) is by far the most common tuning on the 5-string banjo and is used exclusively for playing tunes in the key of G. Many common licks, scales and backup ideas used in Bluegrass music can be adapted for use here. All key of G tunes in this book are arranged in standard G-tuning. Occasionally G-modal tuning (**gDGCD**) is been used for a certain tunes. This tuning involves raising the second string from a B to a C. The primary disadvantage is that the chords and scales will have to be relearned. This tuning tends to work better in clawhammer and other "old timey" tunes than for more scale intensive arrangements. No examples of this approach are shown in this book.

Key of A

For this key, G tuning capoed on the second fret is the most common approach and allows for all key of G chords, scales and licks to be used. All of the key of A tunes in this book have at least one arrangement in this tuning.

It is also possible to play in the key of A in G tuning without a capo. This approach works best with tunes in mixolydian mode where the chord structure includes a predominance of A and G chords. An arrangement of *Red -haired Boy #2* is given to show how this works. There are advantages and disadvantages involved with this approach, however, that need to be understood in order to gain fluency with this technique. One advantage is the absence of a capo, thus eliminating the common frantic capo changing that occurs between tunes in a medley. The greatest disadvantage is that the fifth string will need to be avoided especially when playing chords. This is also a problem since it eliminates a number of common roll patterns and licks that involve the fifth string. Another disadvantage is that the I, IV and V chords (A, D and E) become slightly more awkward than when playing in G tuning with a capo. If you are up to these challenges, you will find some interesting sounds using this approach.

Key of C

When playing in the key of C it is very common to use open G tuning with the capo on the fifth fret. This method has all the advantages of playing in open G. The only disadvantage would be that much of the fingering takes place high up the neck. This can lead to some degree of disorientation 'up there' so it is recommended that you practice with a capo in order to become comfortable in such a position. This also holds true for A, B♭, B and any other key with which a capo is used. This approach works best for arrangements that rely primarily on Bluegrass licks. *Old Dan Tucker #3* and *Billy in the Lowground #1* are good examples of this approach.

It is also common to play in the key of C in G tuning without the use of a capo. *Billy in the Lowground #2* and *Cotton Patch Rag #1* are examples of this approach. With this approach the C major scale, like the G major scale, is relatively easy to manipulate.

Two additional techniques are occasionally used for the key of C. The first of these involves C tuning (**gCGBD**). As long as the melody does not drop below the lowest C note, melodies can be played an octave lower than usual. This advantage is offset by the fact that chords will have to be relearned to accommodate the tuning change. However, by avoiding the fourth string (or C string), standard G tuning chords can be played.

Finally, if the fourth string is lowered to C, and the second string is raised to a C, the result is double C tuning (**gCGCD**). Double C tuning is rarely used outside of clawhammer style due to the disadvantage of having to relearn the neck. This approach can be heard on *Old Dan Tucker 1*.

Key of D

The key of D contains more approaches to playing the banjo than perhaps any other key. The first of these approaches involves placement of the capo on the seventh fret. Like the keys of A and C, the key of D uses G tuning chords, licks, rolls and scales. Again the primary disadvantage is the small amount of neck left for fingering. For an example of this technique see *Green Willis 1*.

Another approach is D tuning (**aDF♯AD**) which can be very effective for playing in the key of D. See *Whiskey Before Breakfast 2* and *Saint Anne's Reel 2* for examples of this technique. For tunes that are strictly melodic, the D major scale is not quite as accessible in this tuning. In addition, chords need to be constructed differently than when playing in G tuning. A common disadvantage with this tuning is that the banjo tends to be more difficult to fine tune. If the banjo is not fine tuned, it will not match other instruments in an ensemble. A high quality electronic tuner can simplify the tuning process and is especially useful during a performance. An advantage of D tuning is that it offers an assortment of licks and sounds that work well when playing typical 3-finger roll patterns.

A second type of D tuning (**f♯DF♯AD**), which is a variation of the D tuning above, allows the D major scale to lie out quite nicely. However, the fourth string (**F♯**) can be a bit burdensome since it turns the IV (or G) chord into a major-seventh that may sound a bit more 'jazzy' than desired. If a tune does not contain IV chords, this tuning can be very advantageous.

And finally, another common technique is C tuning with the capo placed on the second fret. The advantages and disadvantages mentioned for the open C tuning pertain here as well. For examples of this approach see *Forked Deer 2*, *Liberty 2* and *Mississippi Sawyer 2*.

Key of F

It is relatively common for many banjo players to play in the key of F out of open G tuning. *Beaumont Rag 2* is a good example of this. Another option is to remain in G tuning except with the fifth string tuned to an A. Another technique is to use the key of C options except with the capo on the fifth fret. See *Beaumont Rag 1* for an example of this. A final approach includes the same options as found in the key of D except with the capo on the third fret. There are no examples of this approach in the book.

Key of B♭

For the key of B♭, banjo players typically use G tuning with the capo on the third fret. *President Garfield's Hornpipe 1* and *President Garfield's Hornpipe 2* are arranged this way. It is also possible to use B♭ tuning (**fDFB♭D**). *President Garfield's Hornpipe 3* is an example of this approach. Once again the same disadvantages are present here that exist in other tunings (D, double C, etc.).

Key of Dm

Although the key of Dm (as well as other minor keys like Am and Em) can be played in open G tuning, minor tunings can present some interesting possibilities. Dm tuning (**fDFAD**) is a great choice for many tunes in Dm. However, though seemingly unusual, Cm tuning (**gCGCE♭**) with the capo on the second fret presents a remarkably smooth way to play many tunes in Dm. This approach turns a rather difficult piece into an arrangement that 'lies right out' on the fingerboard.

Other Useful Tunings

Gm tuning (**gDGB♭D**) is not only excellent for the key of Gm, but is also good for the relative major key of B♭. This tuning can also be used with the capo on the second fret for playing in the key of Am.

Bm tuning (f♯DF♯BD) is useful for some tunes in the key of Bm as well for the relative major key of D. The only drawback with this tuning is that the IV chord becomes a major-seventh rather that a standard triad.

Gmaj7 tuning (f♯DGBD) is useful for playing in the key of Bm and, with some slight re-tuning, can also be used for the key of D where there is no IV chord.

There are many musical reasons for choosing various tunings for the melodies played on the banjo. For many banjo players however, there are non-musical reasons to approach a tune in a particular way. One of these reasons is that many banjo players like to be able to play in various keys without using a capo.

If you are a beginner you should realize that most experienced players will usually settle on one or two good ways to play in a given key. This 'good way' will vary based on the player's style and preferences. It will also allow the player to get comfortable with chords and licks peculiar to the given approach. Some banjo players are as comfortable playing in the key of C in G tuning as they are in standard key of G. Many others are quite comfortable playing in the key of D in G tuning (with the fifth string tuned to A). This familiarity will also come to you after you have learned enough melodies in a particular tuning and key. With consistent practice any of these approaches will become comfortable to you.

Scales and Chord Inversions

The scales found in the following pages are structured in four different tunings. These scales will be helpful as you increase your familiarity with the various tunings mentioned above.

The chord diagrams in the following pages show major and minor inversions for the G, D B♭ and C minor tunings used in this book. Any major or minor chord can be found by moving the shapes up or down the fingerboard to the appropriate location. These chords cans be used for accompaniment, arranging or improvisation.

Old Time Banjo Style

Some of the banjo parts recorded on the 50 Tunes CD set have been arranged in an old time style called "clawhammer." Rather than mix these parts with the three-finger styles in the body of this book, it seemed a good idea to categorize them together in this appendix instead. The following people are responsible for the recorded version of the listed clawhammer parts:

Rick Davis: *Cripple Creek* and *Cotton Eyed Joe*. Rick does his clawhammer or "up-picking" style with fingerpicks.

Geoff Groberg: *Old Joe Clark* and *Old Dan Tucker*. Geoff also uses a unique, pick free, old time three-finger style on Leather Britches.

Erik Neilson: *Cluck Old Hen* and *Eighth of January*. Erik uses both standard frailing and drop thumb frailing on these tunes.

Note: Clawhammer, frailing and up-picking are all often lumped together under the term 'clawhammer.'

Chord Sequences

The final section of this appendix contains the chord sequences for every tune in this book. It some cases these sequences show the chords as used with a capo. This is because some banjo and guitar parts were recorded with use of a capo. For the most part you should find the chord sequence you need, depending on your use of a capo or any special tunings.

How to Read Tablature

1. The five lines on a tablature staff represent the five strings of the banjo.

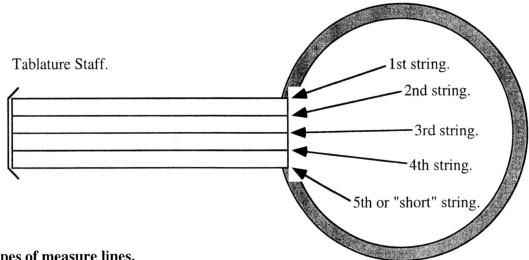

Tablature Staff.

1st string.
2nd string.
3rd string.
4th string.
5th or "short" string.

2. Types of measure lines.

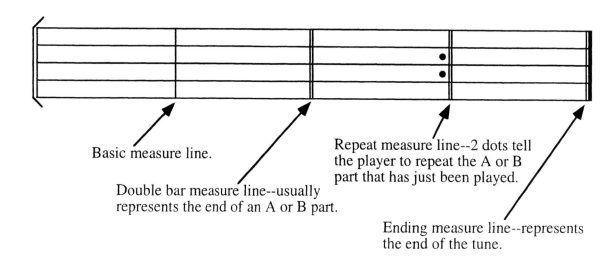

Basic measure line.

Double bar measure line--usually represents the end of an A or B part.

Repeat measure line--2 dots tell the player to repeat the A or B part that has just been played.

Ending measure line--represents the end of the tune.

3. Tablature staff numbers represent fret to be fingered.

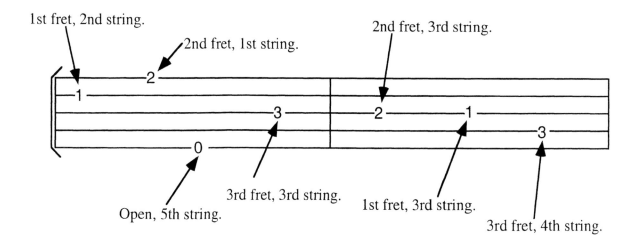

1st fret, 2nd string.

2nd fret, 1st string.

2nd fret, 3rd string.

Open, 5th string.

3rd fret, 3rd string.

1st fret, 3rd string.

3rd fret, 4th string.

4. Stems, beams and note values.

Eighth (8th) notes (8th notes are fast notes).

Quarter note. (A quarter note is a medium-length note).

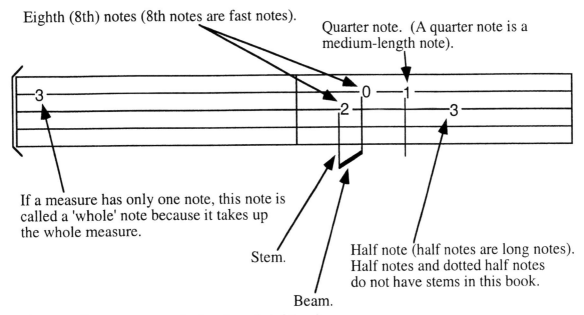

If a measure has only one note, this note is called a 'whole' note because it takes up the whole measure.

Stem.

Beam.

Half note (half notes are long notes). Half notes and dotted half notes do not have stems in this book.

5. Rests (a rest tells you to stop playing for a brief time).

Half note (it takes up half of the measure).

Flag

Eighth note.

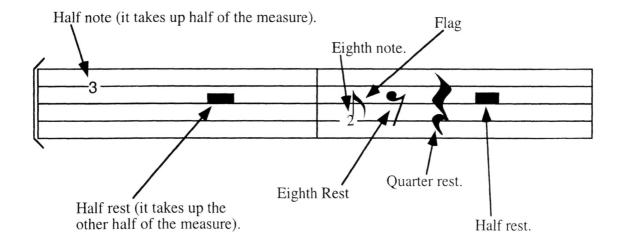

Half rest (it takes up the other half of the measure).

Eighth Rest

Quarter rest.

Half rest.

6. Numbers above notes represent which finger is to play the note below.

2nd finger (plays the note: 3rd fret, 2nd string).

1st finger.

2nd finger.

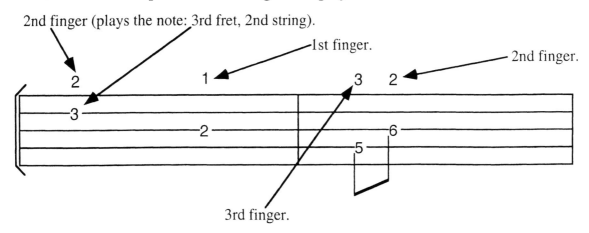

3rd finger.

127

Banjo Roll Exercises

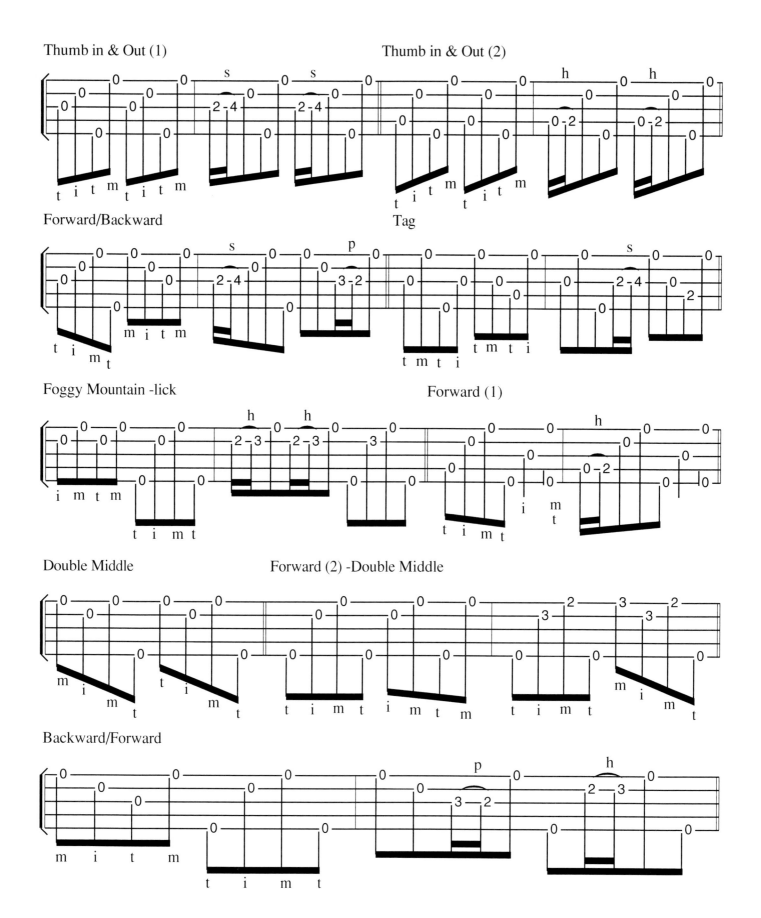

Major Scales

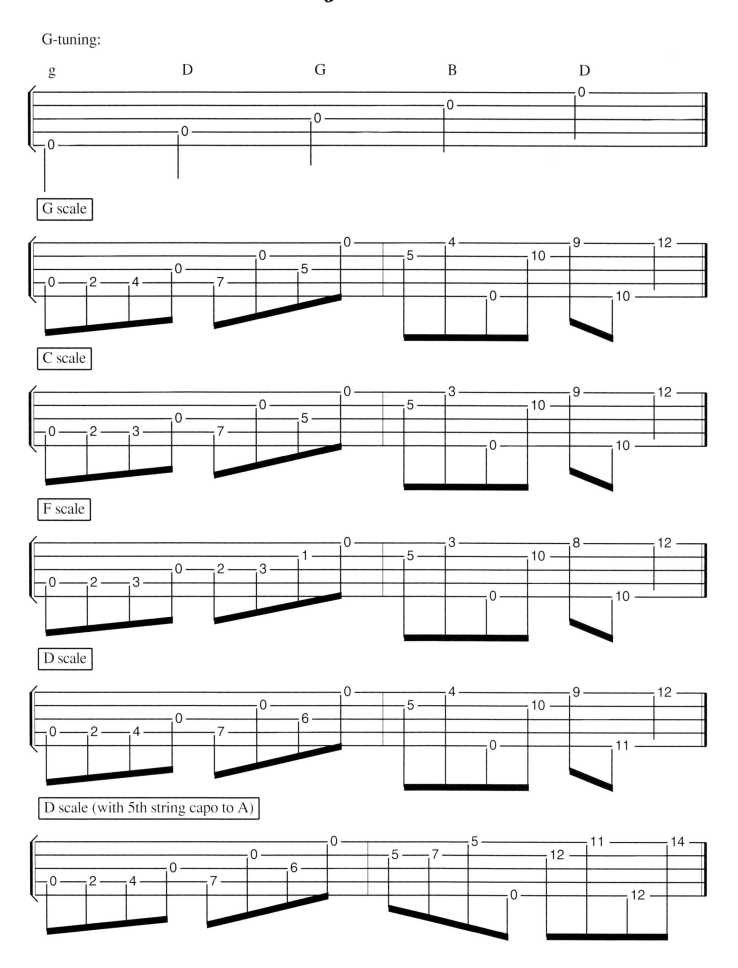

Major Scales (cont.)

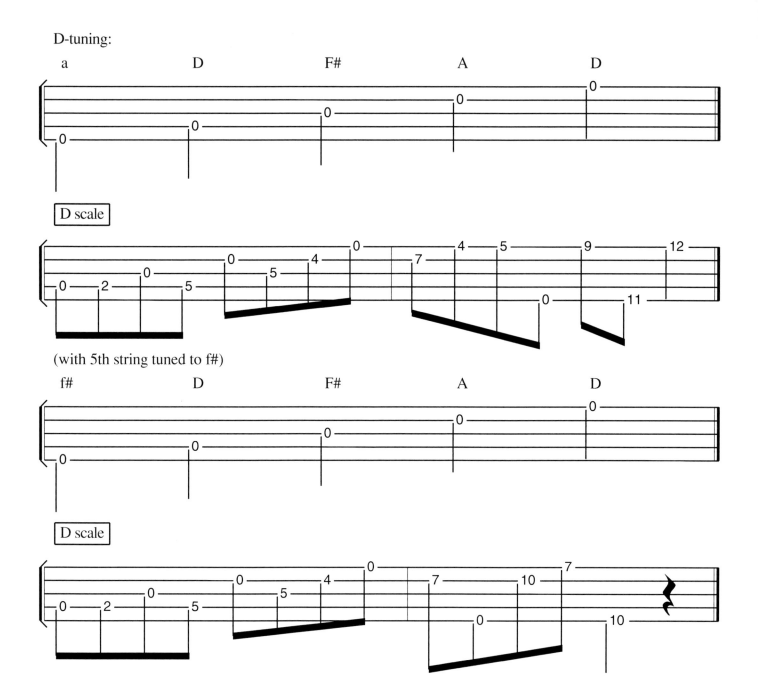

Major Scales (cont.)

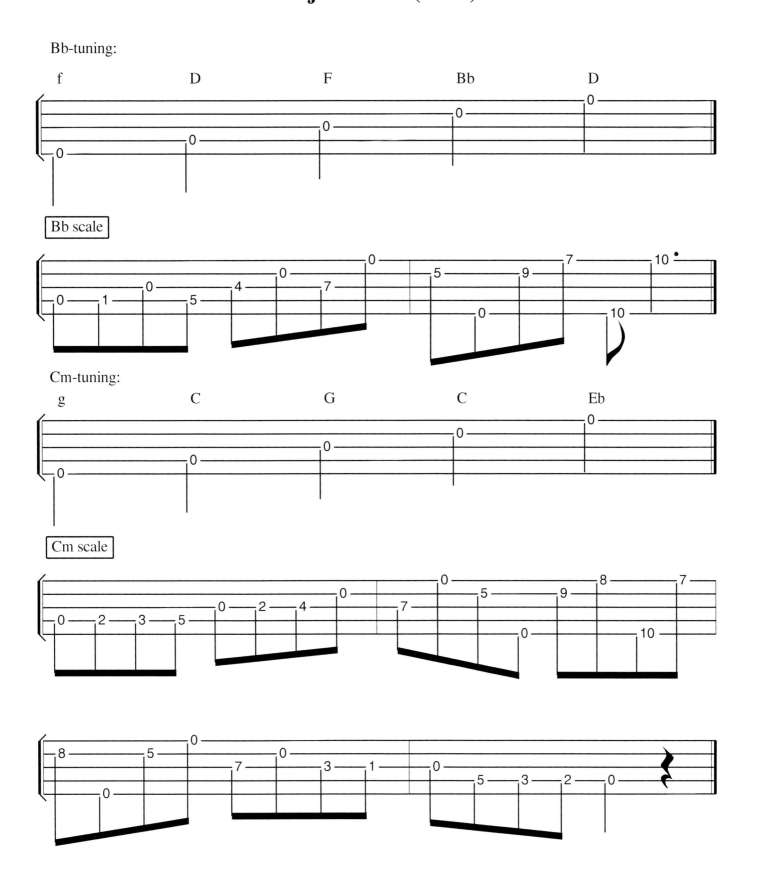

Cluck Old Hen (old-time)

Banjo (capo 2)

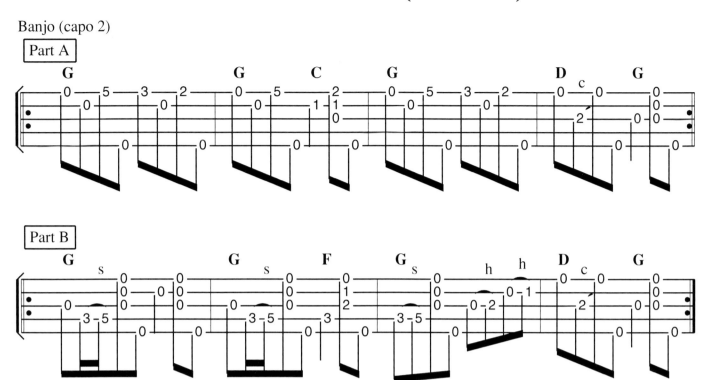

Cotton-eyed Joe (old-time)

Banjo (capo 2)

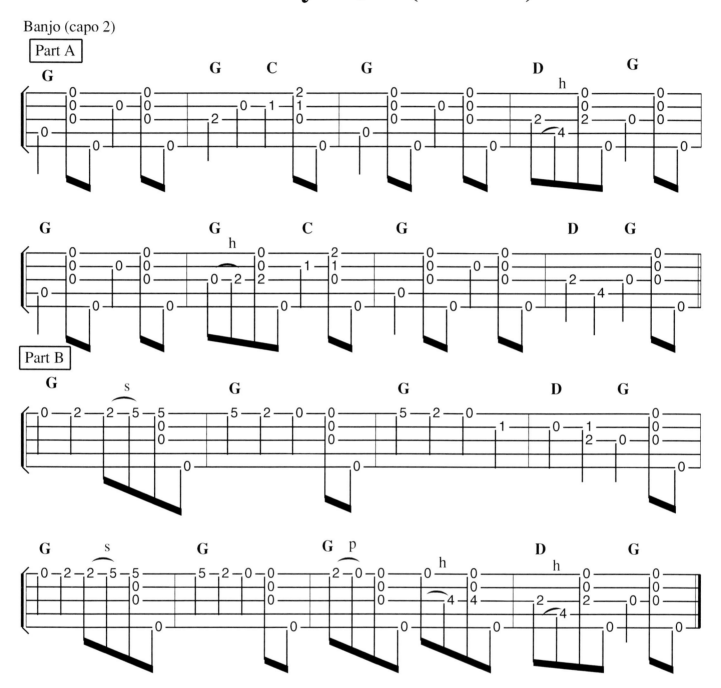

Cripple Creek (old-time)

Banjo (capo 2)

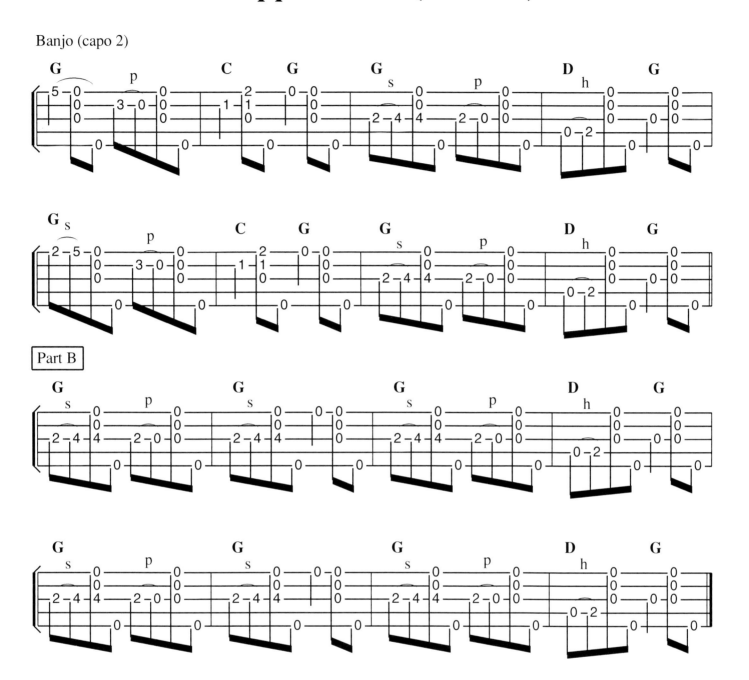

Part B

Eighth of January (old-time)

Banjo 1 (*) (capo 2)

Part A

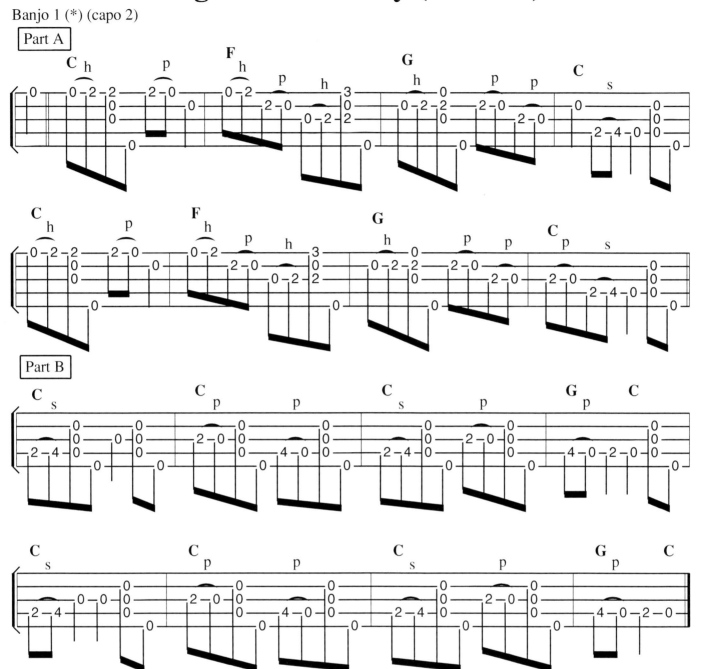

Part B

* Tune banjo: gCGCD (double C tuning)

137

Eighth of January (old-time)

Banjo 2 (*) (capo 2)

Part A

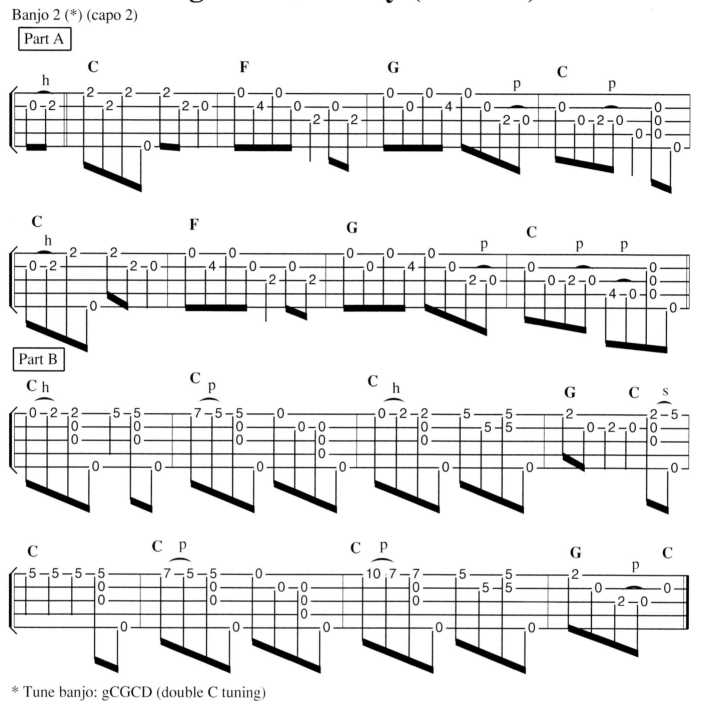

Part B

* Tune banjo: gCGCD (double C tuning)

Leather Britches (old-time)

Banjo

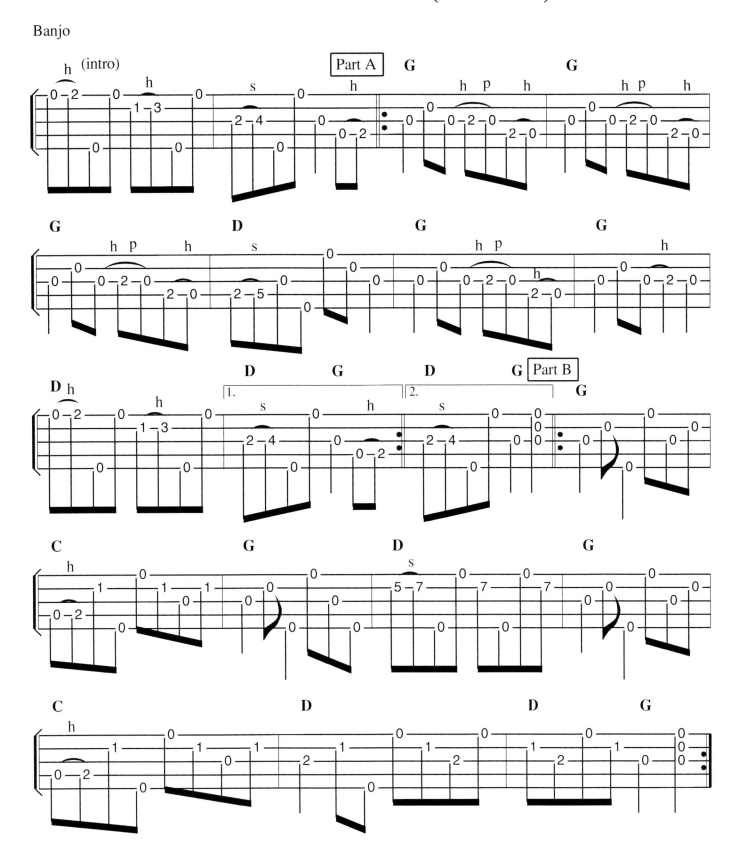

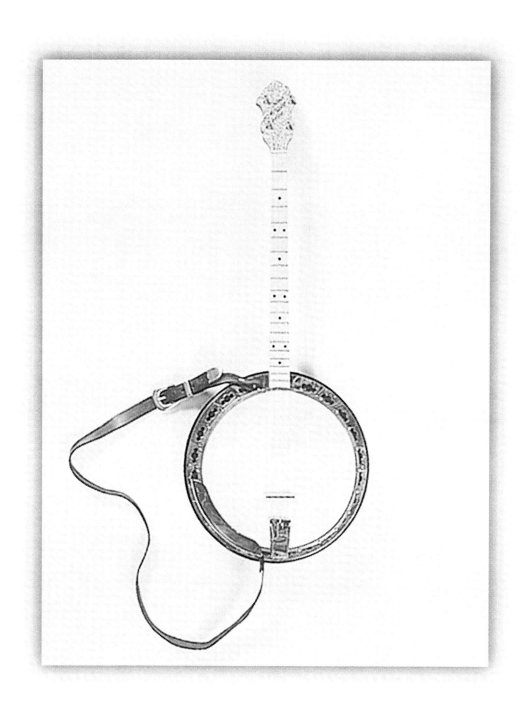

Old Dan Tucker (old-time)

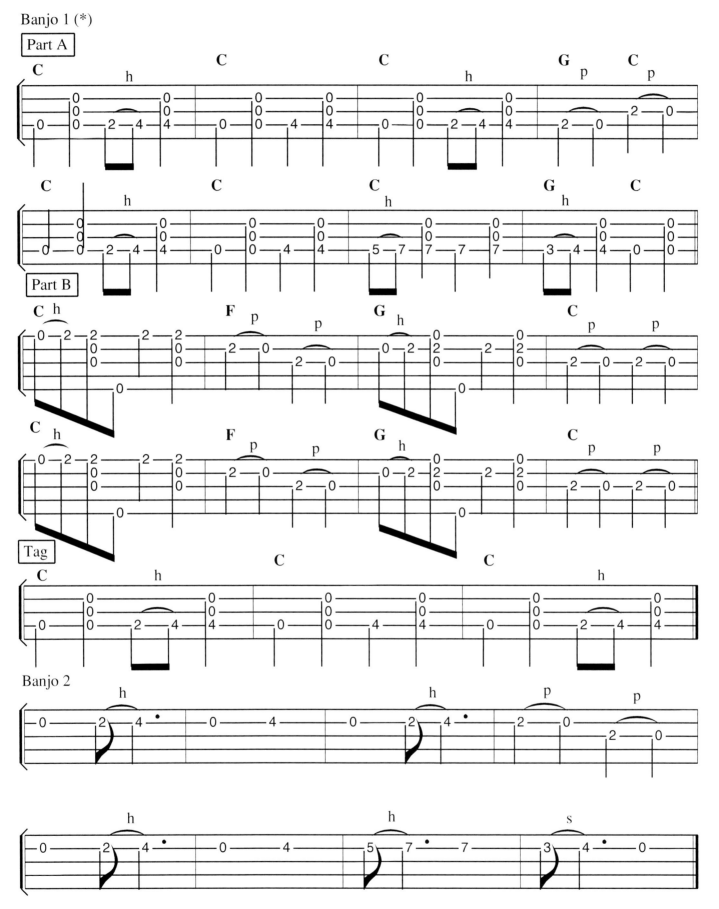

*Tune banjo: gCGCD (double C tuning)

Old Joe Clark (old-time)

Banjo (capo 2)

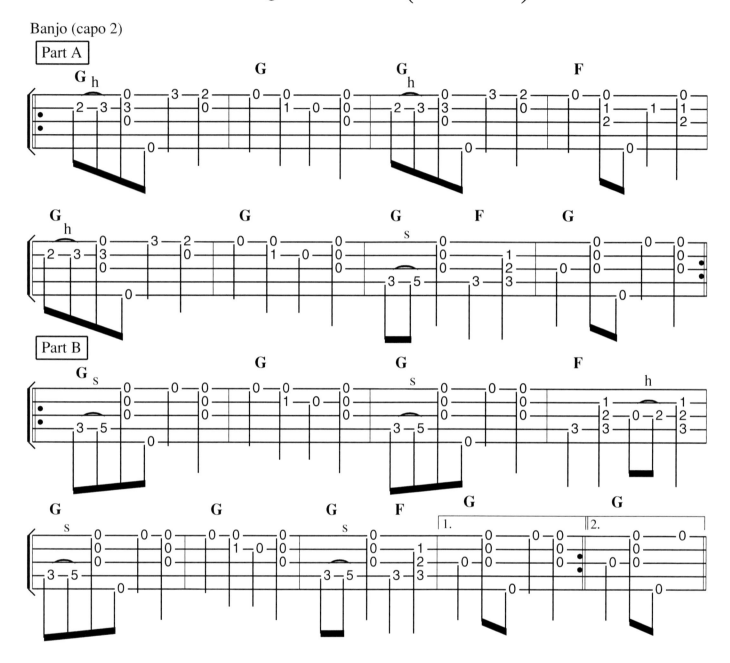

Open Chords in G-tuning

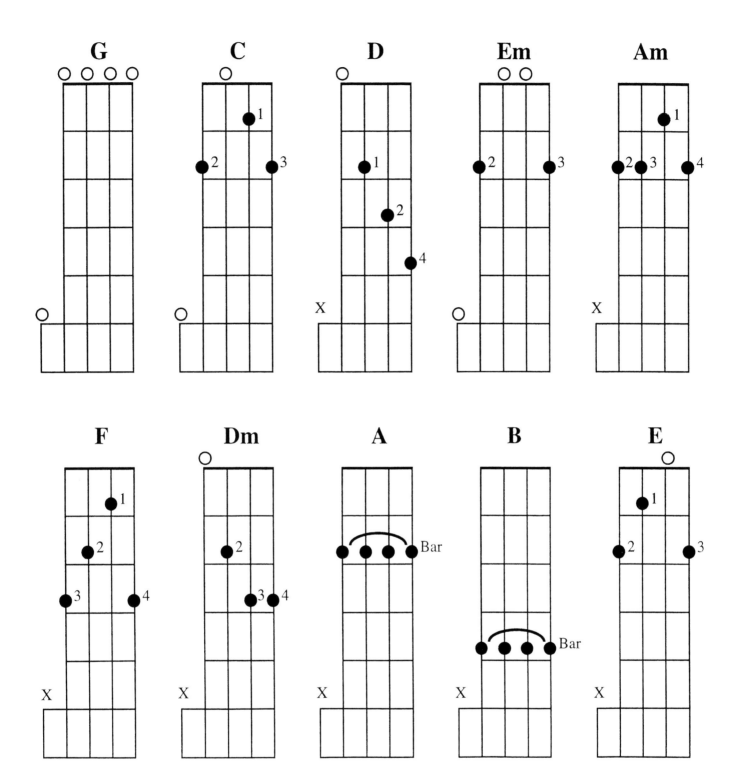

Chord Inversions in G-tuning (major)

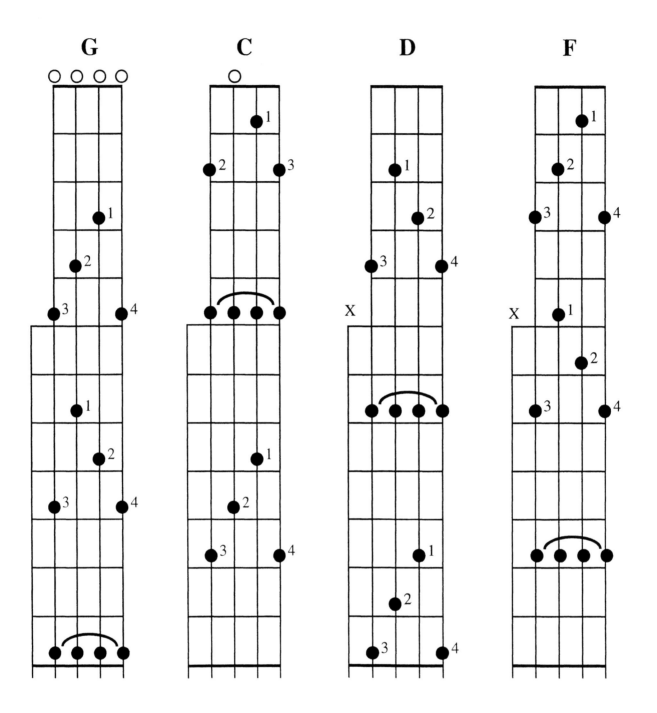

Chord Inversions in G-tuning (minor)

Em   Am   Bm

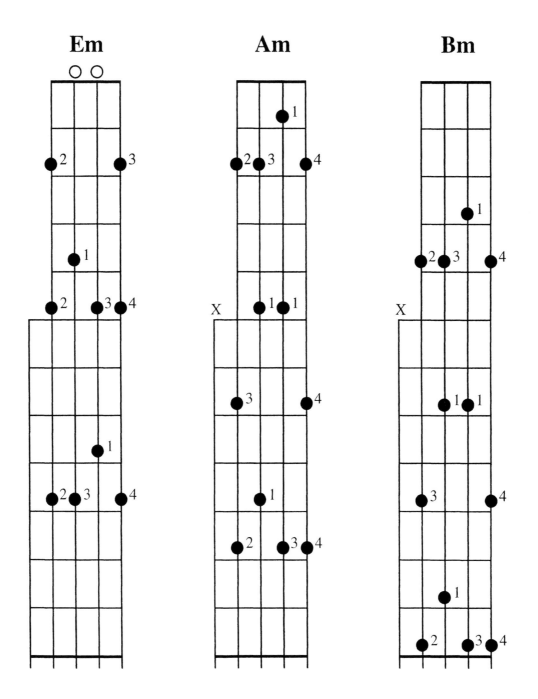

Chord Inversions in D-tuning (major)

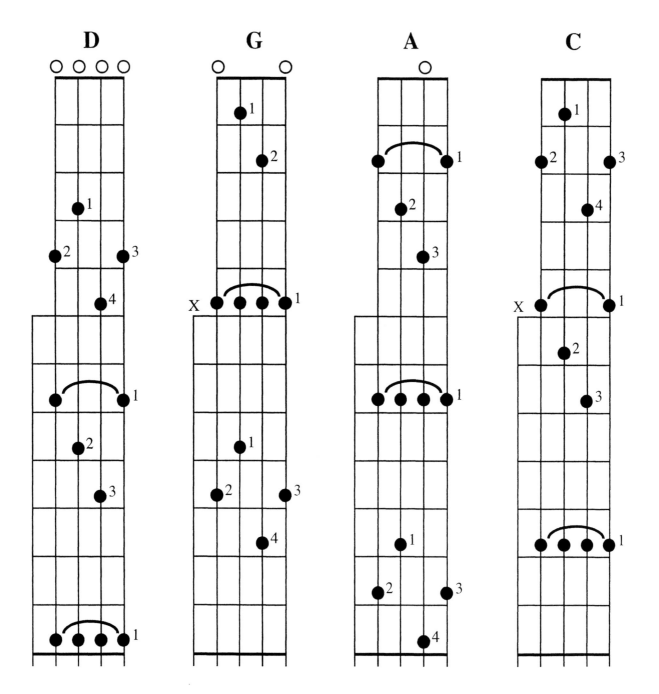

Chord Inversions in D-tuning (minor)

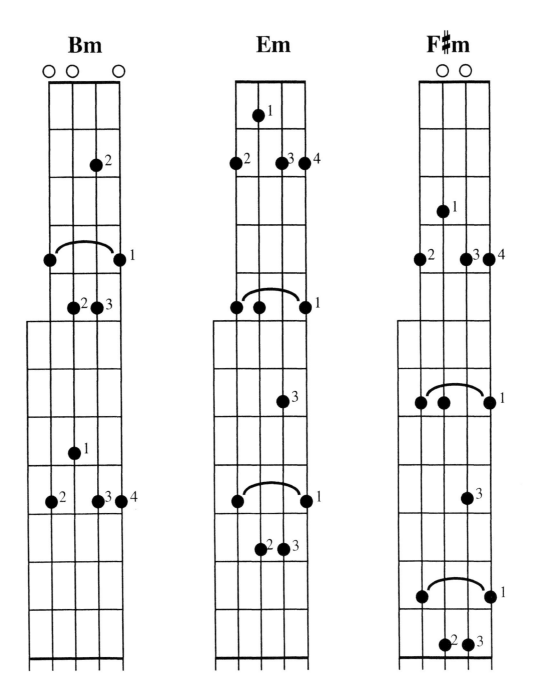

Chord Inversions in B♭-tuning (major)

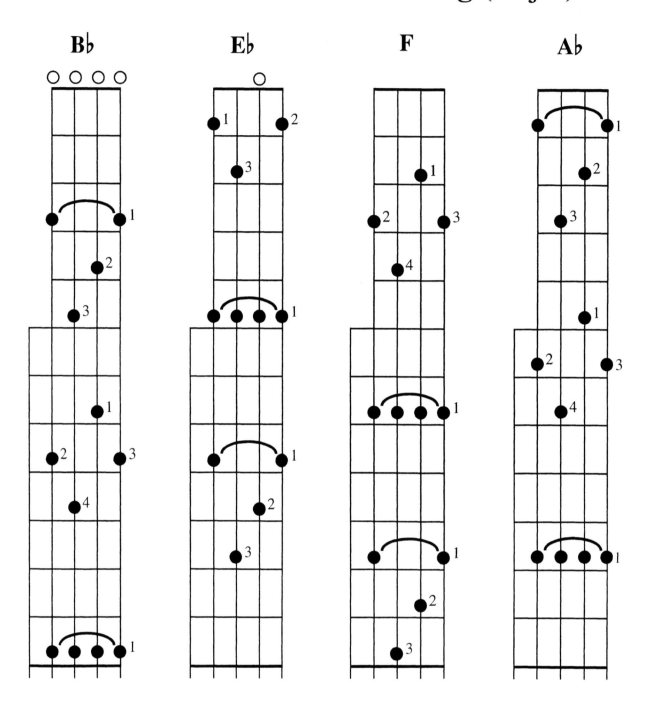

Chord Inversions in B♭-tuning (minor)

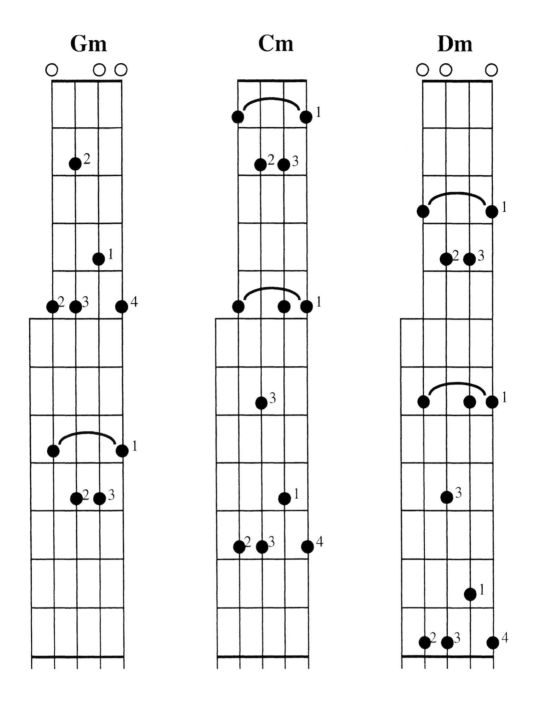

Chord Inversions in Cm-tuning (major)

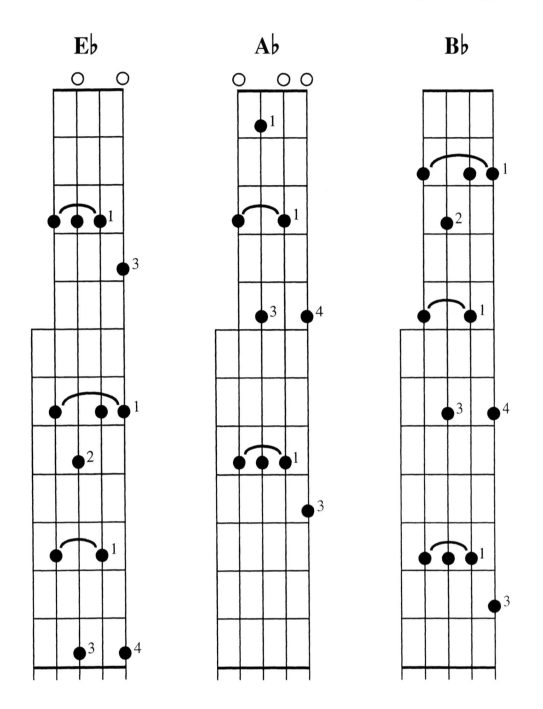

Chord Inversions in Cm-tuning

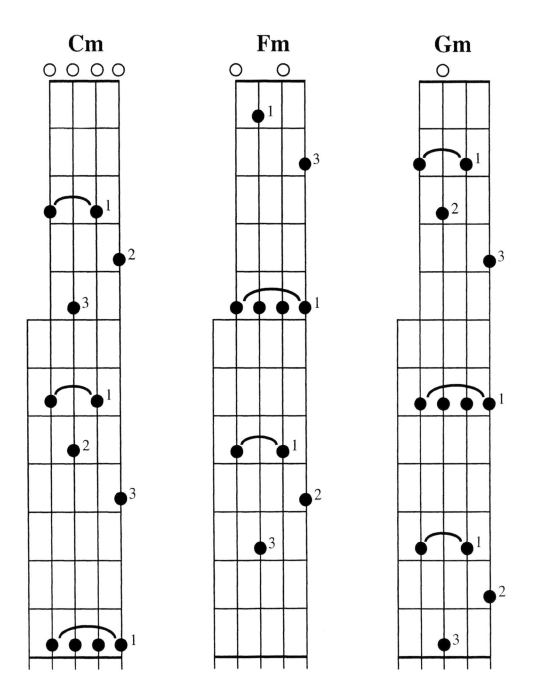

Angus Campbell

Chords
Part A
|: A | A | D A | E |
| A | A | D A | E A :|

Part B
|: A | A | E | E |
| A | A | D A | E A :|

(capo 2)
Part A
|: G | G | C G | D |
| G | G | C G | D G :|

Part B
|: G | G | D | D |
| G | G | C G | D G :|

Arkansas Traveler

Chords
Part A (key of D)
|: D Bm | A D | A | A | D Bm | A D | D G | A D :|

Part B
|: D G | D A | D A | Bm A | D G | D A | D G | A D :|

Fiddle, Mandolin & Bass
Part A (key of C)
|: C Am | G C | G | G | C Am | G C | C F | G C :|

Part B
|: C F | C G | C G | Am G | C F | C G | C F | G C :|

Guitar will use these chords
Part A (key of G –Banjo solo)
|: G Em | D G | D | D | G Em | D G | G C | D G :|

Part B
|: G C | G D | G D | Em D | G C | G D | G C | D G :|

Aura Lee

Chords
4/4
Part A
|: A | D | E7 | A :|

Part B
| A C#7 | F#m |
| D Dm | A |
| A C#o Bm F#m |
| B7 | Bm7 E7 | A |

The Battle Cry of Freedom

Chords
Key of F
Part A
| F | F | B♭ | B♭ | F | F | F | C |
| F | F | B♭ | B♭ | F | F | C | F |

Part B
| F | B♭ | F | F | F | B♭ | F | C |
| F | F | B♭ | B♭ | F | F | C | F |

(capo 5) for Key of F (C position)
Part A
| C | C | F | F | C | C | C | G | C | C | F | F | C | C | G | C |

Part B
| C | F | C | C | C | F | C | G | C | C | F | F | C | C | G | C |

Key of G
Part A
| G | G | C | C | G | G | G | D |
| G | G | C | C | G | G | D | G |

Part B
| G | C | G | G | G | C | G | D |
| G | G | C | C | G | G | D | G |

Beaumont Rag

Chords
Key of F
Parts A & B

: C7	C7	F	F
C7	C7	F	F
C7	C7	F	F7
B♭	F D7	G7 C7	F :

Key of C
Parts A & B

: G7	G7	C	C
G7	G7	C	C
G7	G7	C	C7
F	C A7	D7 G7	C :

Billy in the Lowground

Chords
Part A

|: C | C | Am | Am |
| C | C | Am | G C :|

Part B

|: C | C | Am | F |
| C | C | Am | G C :|

Blackberry Blossom

Chords
Part A

|: G D | C G | C G | A D |
| G D | C G | C G | D G :|

Part B

|: Em | Em | Em | B7 |
| Em | Em | C G | D G :|

Bonaparte's Retreat

Chords
Part A

|: D | D | D | D :|

Part B (melody 1 -simple)

| D | D | A | A |
| D | D | A | D |

Part B (melody 2 -fancy)

|: D | A | D | A D :|

Carthage Waltz

Chords
Part A

G	D	C	G
Am	Bm	Am7	D
G	*D D G	Am7	D

Part B

*G C C	G	*G D D	G
G	C	G	Em
Am	G	D	G

*1 strum per chord (all other chords:
pick/strum/strum)

Cherokee Shuffle

Chords
Part A

|: A | A | A | F♯m |
| D | A | D E | A :|

Part B

|: D | A | D | A | D | A |
| A | F♯m | D E | A :|

(capo 2)
Part A

|: G | G | G | Em |
| C | G | C D | G :|

Part B

|: C | G | C | G | C | G |
| G | Em | C D | G :|

Cluck Old Hen

Chords
Part A

|: A | A D | A | E A :|

Part B

|: A | A G | A | E A :|

(capo 2)
Part A

|: G | G C | G | D G :|

Part B

|: G | G F | G | D G :|

Cotton-eyed Joe

Chords
Key of A
Part A

|: A | A D | A | E A :|

Part B

|: A | A | A | E A :|

Key of G (or Capo 2 for key of A)
Part A

|: G | G C | G | D G :|

Part B

|: G | G | G | D G :|

Key of D
Part A

|: D | D G | D | A D :|

Part B

|: D | D | D | A D :|

Cotton Patch Rag

Chords
Parts A & E

| C | C7 | F F/E | F/E♭ D | G | G | C | G |
| C | C7 | F F/E | F/E♭ D | G | G | G | C |

Part B (can be used as Parts A and B
for Guitar, Mandolin & Banjo)

| C | C7 | F | F | G | G | C | G |
| C | C7 | F | F | G | G | G | C |

Part C

| Am | Am | Dm | Dm | G | G | C | G |
| Am | Am | Dm | Dm | G | G | G | C |

Part D

| A7 | A7 | D7 | D7 | G | G | C | G |
| A7 | A7 | D7 | D7 | G | G | G | C |

Part F

| C | C | B | B | Dm | Dm | C | G |
| C | C | B | B | Dm | Dm | G | C |

Cripple Creek

Chords
Part A

|: A | D A | A | E A :|

Part B

|: A | A | A | E A :|

(capo 2)
Part A

|: G | C G | G | D G :|

Part B

|: G | G | G | D G :|

Devil's Dream

Chords
Part A & B (key of D)

|: D | D | Em | Em |
| D | D | G D | A D :|

Fiddle parts
Parts A & B (key of G)

|: G | G | Am | Am |
| G | G | C G | D G :|

Guitar and 1st Mandolin part
Parts A & B (key of A)

|: A | A | Bm | Bm |
| A | A | D A | E A :|

2nd Mandolin part
For chords on Banjo, use key of G chords
(w/capo 2 for key of A)

Down Yonder

Chords

G	G	G	G
C	C	C	C
G	G	G	G
G	G	G	G
A	A	A	A
D (tacet)	(cont.)	D (tacet)	(cont.)
G	G	G	G
C	C	C	C
G	G	G	G
A	D	G	G

Eighth of January

Chords
Key of D
Part A

|: D | G | A | D :|

Part B

|: D | D | D | A D :|

(capo 2)
Part A

|: C | F | G | C :|

Part B

|: C | C | C | G C :|

Chords (Texas-style)
Key of D
Part A

|: D | G | A | D :|

Part B

D F#o	G G#o	D	A D
D F#o	G G#o
A Bo	C#o D

(capo 2)
Part A

|: C | F | G | C :|

Part B

| C Eo | F F#o | C | G |
| C Eo | F F#o | G Ao | Bo C |

155

Forked Deer

Chords
Part A

|: D | G A | D | A |
| D | G A | D G | A D :|

Part B

|: A | A | A | D |
| A | A | D G | A D :|

(capo 2)
Part A

|: C | F G | C | G |
| C | F G | C F | G C :|

Part B

|: G | G | G | C |
| G | G | C F | G C :|

Gardenia Waltz

Chords
3/4
Key of G (1st part)

G	Bm	Em	G	G	Bm	Am7	D
Am	AmM7	Am7	Am6
D	D+	G	D
G	Bm	Em	G	G	G7	C	Am
C	Cm	G	E7	Am7	D	G	G

Key of D (2nd part)

D	Bm	F♯m	Bm	D	D♯o
Em7	A7	Em	C	D	A7	A
A/C♯	D	A
D	Bm	F♯m	Bm	D	D7	G
Em	G	Gm	D	B7	Em7	A7
D	D

Grandfather's Clock

Chords
Part A

|G|D|G|C|G|D|G|D||G|D|G|C|G|D|G|G|

Part B

G	G	C	G
G	Em	Am7	D
G	D	G	C	G	D	G	G

Part C (Banjo)

|: G | C G | G (tacet) | (tacet cont.) :|
| G | D | G | C | G | D | G | G |

Green Willis

Chords
Part A

:D | D | A | E A |
| D | D | A | D :|

Part B

|: D | D | Em | A |
| D | D G | A | D :|

(capo 2)
Part A

|: C | C | G | D G |
| C | C | G | C :|

Part B

|: C | C | Dm | G |
| C | C F | G | C :|

156

Indian's Farewell Waltz

Chords
Part A

Dm	Gm	Gm	A
C	C	Dm	A
Dm	C	Dm	Gm
Dm	A	Dm	Dm

Part B

| F | C | F | Gm |
| Dm | C | Dm | Dm |

(capo 5)
Part A

Am	Dm	Dm	E
G	G	Am	E
Am	G	Am	Dm
Am	E	Am	Am

Part B

| C | G | C | Dm |
| Am | G | Am | Am |

Irish Washerwoman

Chords (6/8)
Part A

|: G | G | D | D |
| G | G | C D | G :|

Part B

: G	G	D	D
C G	C G
C D	G :

La Bastringue

Chords
Part A

: D	A D	A	D
D	A D
G	A D :

Part B (repeat 1st line 2 times)

|: D | C | D | A D :|
| D | C | D G | A D |

Leather Britches

Chords
Part A

|: G | G | G | D |
| G | G | D | D G :|

Part B

|: G | C | G | D |
| G | C | D | D G :|

Texas-style
Parts A & B

: G Bo	C7 C♯o
G Bo	D
G Bo	C7 C♯o
D Eo	F♯o G :

Liberty

Chords
Part A

|: D | D | G | G |
| D | D | A | D :|

Part B

|: D | D | D | A |
| D | D | A | D :|

(capo 2)
Part A

|: C | C | F | F |
| C | C | G | C :|

Part B

|: C | C | C | G |
| C | C | G | C :|

Martin's Waltz

Chords
3/4
Part A

D	F♯7	G	E7
A7	A7	D	A7
D	F♯7	G	E7
A7	A7	D	D

Part B

A	C♯m	F♯m	A
E7	E7	A	E7
A	C♯m	F♯m	A
E7	E7	A	A7	(Return to Part A)

Mason's Apron

Chords
Parts A & B

|: A | A | Bm | Bm |
| A | A | D | E A :|

(capo 2)
Parts A & B

|: G | G | Am | Am |
| G | G | C | D G :|

Mississippi Hornpipe

Chords
Part A

|: G | C | G | D |
| G | C | D | G :|

Part B

: G D	Em Bm
C G	Am D
G D	Em Bm
C G	D G :

Mississippi Sawyer

Chords
Part A

|: D | D | G | G |
| D | D | A | D :|

Part B

|: D | D | A | A |
| D | D | A | D :|

Old Dan Tucker

Chords
Part A
|: C | C | C | G C :|
Part B
|: C | F | G | C :|

Old Joe Clark

Chords
Parts A & B
|: A | A | A | G |
| A | A | A G | A :|
(capo 2)
Parts A & B
|: G | G | G | F |
| G | G | G F | G :|

President Garfield's Hornpipe

Chords
Part A
|: B♭ | B♭ | F | F |
| B♭ | B♭ | F | B♭ :|
Part B
|: E♭ | B♭ | F | B♭ |
| E♭ | B♭ | F | B♭ :|
(capo 3)
Part A
|: G | G | D | D |
| G | G | D | G :|
Part B
|: C | G | D | G |
| C | G | D | G :|

Pretty Peg

Chords
Part A
| D | D A | Bm | A |
| Bm A | G A | G | A |
Part B
D D/C♯	D/B A	D	D A
D D/C♯	D/B A
Bm G	A D
(capo 2)
Part A
| C | C G | Am | G | Am G | F G | F | G |
Part B
| C C/B | Am G | C | C G |
| C C/B | Am G | Am F | G C |

Red-haired Boy

Chords
Part A
|: A | A D | A | G |
| A | A D | A | E A :|
Part B
|: G | D | A | G |
| A | A D | A | E A :|
(capo 2)
Part A
|: G | G C | G | F |
| G | G C | G | D G :|
Part B
|: F | C | G | F |
| G | G C | G | D G :|

Red Wing

Chords
Part A

G	G	C	G
D	G	A	D
G	G	C	G
D	G	AD	G

Part B

C	C	G	G
D	D	G	G7
C	C	G	G
D	D	G	G

College Hornpipe

Chords
Part A

|:Bb|Bb|C|F|
|Bb Do|D#7 Eo|F|Bb:|

Part B

|:Bb|Eb|C|F|
|Bb Do|D#7 Eo|F|Bb:|

(capo 3)
Part A

|:G|G|A|D|
|G Bo|C7 C#o|D|G:|

Part B

|:G|C|A|D|
|G Bo|C7 C#o|D|G:|

Sailor's Hornpipe

Chords
Part A

G	G	A	D
G Em	C Am
G D	G

Part B

G	C	A	D
G Em	C Am
G D	G

Saint Anne's Reel

Chords
Part A

|:D|D|G|D|
|D|D|GA|D:|

Part B

|:D|Em|A|D|
|Bm|Em|A|D:|

(capo 2)
Part A

|:C|C|F|C|
|C|C|FG|C:|

Part B

|:C|Dm|G|C|
|Am|Dm|G|C:|

Sally Ann

Chords
Part A

|: A | D | D | A |
| A | Bm | E | A :|

Part B (repeat 3 times)

|: A | Bm | E | A :|

(capo 2)
Part A

|: G | C | C | G |
| G | Am | D | G :|

Part B (repeat 3 times)

|: G | Am | D | G :|

Sally Goodin'

Chords
Parts A & B

|: A | A | A | E A | A | A | A | E A :|

(capo 2)
Parts A & B

|: G | G | G | D G | G | G | G | D G :|

Texas-style
Parts A & B

: A C#o	D7 D#o
A C#o	E
A C#o	D7 D#o
E F#o	G#o A :

(capo 2)
Parts A & B

|: G Bo | C7 C#o | G Bo | D |
| G Bo | C7 C#o | D Eo | F#o G :|

Sally Johnson

Chords
A part

|: G | G | G | D |
| G | G | D | D G :|

B part

|: G | C | G | G Em |
| G | C | D | D G :|

Texas-style
Part A

|: G Bo | C7 C#o | G Bo | Bbo Ao |
| G Bo | C7 C#o | D Eo | F#o G :|

Part B

|: G Bo | C7 C#o | G Bo | G Em |
| G Bo | C7 C#o | D Eo | F#o G :|

Salt Creek

Chords
Part A

|: A | A D | G | G E |
| A | A D | G | E A :|

Part B

|: A | A | G | G |
| A | A | G | E A :|

(capo 2)
Part A

|: G | G C | F | F D |
| G | G C | F | D G :|

Part B

|: G | G | F | F | G | G | F | D G :|

Soldier's Joy

Chords
Part A
|: D | D | D | A |
| D | D | DA | D :|
Part B
|: D | G | D | A |
| D | G | DA | D :|
(capo 2)
Part A
|: C | C | C | G | C | C | CG | C :|
Part B
|: C | F | C | G | C | F | CG | C :|

Swallowtail Jig

Chords
Part A
|: Em | Em | D | D |
| Em | Em | D | Em :|
Part B
: Em	Em
Em	Em D
Em	Em	D	Em :

Temperance Reel

Chords
Part A
|: G | G | Em | Em |
| G | G | Em | D G :|
Part B
: Em	Em	D	D
Em	Em
Em	D G :

Tom & Jerry

Chords
Parts A & B (simple)
|: A | A | A | E | A | A | A | EA :|
Parts A & B (w/D-chord)
|: A | D | A | E | A | D | A | EA :|
Parts A & B (w/E-chord 3rd and 7th measures)
|: A | D | E | E | A | D | E | EA :|
Texas-style
Part A & B
|: A C#o | D7 D#o | A C#o | Co Bo |
| A C#o | D7 D#o | E F#o | G#o A :|
(capo 2)
Parts A & B (simple)
|: G | G | G | D | G | G | G | DG :|
Parts A & B (w/C-chord)
|: G | C | G | D | G | C | G | DG :|
Parts A & B (w/D-chord 3rd and 7th measures)
|: G | C | D | D | G | C | D | DG :|
Texas-style
Part A & B
|: G Bo | C7 C#o | G Bo | Bbo Ao |
| G Bo | C7 C#o | D Eo | F#o G :|

Turkey in the Straw

Chords
Key of G
Part A

|: G | G | G | D |
| G | G | G | D G :|

Part B

|: G | G7 | C | C (C#o)* |
| G | G D | G | D G :|

Key of C
Part A

|: C | C | C | G |
| C | C | C | G C :|

Part B

|: C | C7 | F | F (F#o) |
| C | C G | C | G C :|

*chords in parentheses are optional for the measure (these chords can be heard on CD).

Uncle Joe

Parts A and B

|: D | D | D | A | D | D | G | A :|

Under the Double Eagle

Chords
(Guitar solo)
Part A

|: C | C | C | C | G | G | C | C :|

Part B

C	C	C	C	C	C	G	G
G	G	G	G	G	G	C	C
C	C	C	C	C	C7	F	F
F	G#	C	A7	D7	G7	C* C#	D

(Mandolin solo)
Part A

|: G | G | G | G | D | D | G | G :|

Part B

C	C	C	C	C	C	G	G
G	G	G	G	G	G	C	C
C	C	C	C	C	C7	F	F
F	Fm	C	A7	D7	G7	C	C

*If you decide not to change to key of G, end on C chord.

Whiskey Before Breakfast

Chords
Part A

|: D | D | G D | A |
| D | D | G D | A D :|

Part B

|: D | D | Em | A |
| D A | G D | G D | A D :|

(capo 2)
Part A

|: C | C | F C | G |
| C | C | F C | G C :|

Part B

|: C | C | Dm | G |
| C G | F C | F C | G C :|

163